Navigating the Storms of Adolescence: A 30 Day Guidebook to Calmer Waters for Parents

By

L. R. Martens, Ph.D.

Publisher: CreateSpace Independent Publishers

Printed in the United States of America

ISBN-13: 978-1500745035

ISBN-10: 1500745030

For the One Who Taught Me How to Be a Parent:

For My Light, My Son, Drew

4

Order of Contents

Synopsis of
Daily Activities and Resources

PREFACE

This guidebook is designed, in essence, to help reduce the amount of stress encountered when raising children who are in the "sea of adolescence". Ours is a very fast-paced world...more now than ever before. And this pace *really* affects parents who are trying to connect with their children. And, once these children are teenagers, they have their own worlds, too. The need for children to be raised successfully into adulthood vitally important and more complex now than in any previous generation! What we need is a **quick** reference that can act as a guide through a rough spell. The deeper meanings, lengthy techniques, and long explanations can come later from other sources (that are listed in the resource section). My background in science always leads me to the observation that if we gather more information from different sources with different perspectives, we are bound to develop more accurate conclusions. So, if you are in a position to find the time to read these other helpful works, this author thinks that is fantastic! This particular resource is, quite simply, a 30 day guide to restore some level of sanity that has been temporarily misplaced in the rubble of parenting a teen. The background for reading for each day only takes about 15-20 minutes. The activity for each day will vary in time required. Some only take 15 minutes while others may take a day to complete, with an analysis of progress taking place further down the road. In general, the activities will help with communication between parent and child, with some skill-building along the way. In particular, this guidebook is designed to assist in those moments of chaos when you feel that you and your teen are "losing touch" and just need a clearly defined course of action to get back on track.

Once the voyage is accomplished in 30 days, however, I encourage you to revisit many of the activities at a later time. Given that our teenagers are in a state of rapid flux, it will not be surprising if you find, for example, that the answers your children give for the activity on "day 1" change over as short a time period as six months later! Don't be surprised if the symbols you discuss on "day 3" are replaced with other entirely different ones from 8th grade to 10th grade. That is to be expected. Thus, it might also help to keep this guidebook handy for a few years! Fortunately, this book is NOT a five volume, 300 page dissertation on the research of every nook and cranny (sulci and gyri) of a teenager's brain. In fact, a parent dealing with the dilemmas of raising a teenager typically does not have the time to sit and read such volumes. And, even if they did, they might just be better off jumping on a plane heavily loaded with vodka and headed for a two-week retreat at the base of the Himalayas. (If one of these really does exist for such a purpose, please contact me immediately with the address so I can set it in my GPS system.)

Another reason for creating this resource is based not only on my own experiences as a parent of a child who is now grown and out of the nest (insert applause and celebration here), but also observations I have made over 25 years in the classroom working with high school adolescents…and working through issues assisting their parents, as well. One could say that teachers have more anecdotal and longitudinal knowledge about children and children as students (as they ARE different) than any other group of people working with kids. And this information is highly valuable, but undocumented and is usually not organized into a cohesive body of knowledge, much less a philosophy of function and approach that could be offered to other individuals needing the information. This is one of the travesties of the educational system. It does not encourage teachers to respond as researchers in any significant capacity that can be applied in other areas. Thus, data and information are lost to the passing of time from one school year to the next.

Here's a quick illustration of how much knowledge a teacher can provide given one simple scenario. A parent contacts the teacher, concerned because her son has dyed his hair blue. If the teacher has even been in the classroom for, say, ten years…and high school teachers usually have five to six classes of approximately 30 to 40 students each…that would be 9 months of intense, longitudinal observation on 150 to 200 teenagers…in just one school year! Very few researchers could say they have the opportunity to observe 200 case studies every single day for 9 month period, and then repeat that same number of cases every year. After a decade, that teacher has observed 1500 to 2000 teenagers...along with their behaviors, conversations, social interactions, and academic progress. In addition, the teacher is networked into the system for years on end, acutely aware of how many of these kids are doing months and even years later! So, if the teacher doesn't respond with panic and deep concern initially upon seeing this student with blue hair, there is good reason. Blue hair in and of itself is not a crisis. Maybe it is in YOUR home...but not within the classroom when compared to the behaviors of teenagers in general. There will be more detail on this in the chapter on "Teachers".

Another important reason for developing and using this guidebook is that it has very concrete, hands-on activities on a clear, short timeline. And even more critical, the questions developed for these activities vary slightly from many you will see online with other sources for self-help about teens. But the difference in HOW the questions are phrased is very, very potent. And the difference has been derived from observing how teenagers respond to certain phrases...or how they provide dismissive answers to certain ones. For example, many parents ask their children "How was your day at school?" And they frequently get a response like "...Fine" with nothing more. The one we teachers really like is the response to "What did you DO at school today?"....you guessed it...the answer is typically "Nothing". That's right. We did nothing. I just love doing nothing in front of 30 teenagers for an entire class period. It's what I live for. Notice the oh-so-subtle difference between the two scenarios below:

What many parents typically ask:

"What music do you listen to most often?"

What could be asked based on the information in this guide:

"Which three musical artists/groups do you listen to most often? ...and **WHY**? What is it about their music that you like?"

"Name a musical artist that some of your friends listen to ...but YOU can't stand. What about that artist makes you **not** like them?"

"Which musical artist do you listen to when you are sad? ...when you are angry?"

"Which lyrics are most accurate in describing how you see yourself in the world?

Yes, the phrasing proposed in the daily activities of this book changes the depth to which the parent is probing for knowledge about their child. The precision of aligning the question to the desired information is critical. When we look at the first question asked by the parent above, it is not a bad one at all. In fact, it's a good place to start. However, it is very limited in revealing much about the child, and because it is relatively superficial, may even be answered with an *expected* response. Some great readings on the details of phraseology and reasons *behind* the differences can be found in the works of Dr. Michael Riera (2003) as well. Our children know what we want most of the time. But in-depth questions make us think...beyond immediate expectations of others. We tend to reveal more about ourselves in answering these types of questions ...many times more than we realize.

If, after going through the activities in this guidebook, you feel that you know your child and his/her world a little bit better...then the guidebook has achieved its primary purpose. If you walk away from this book with more information to assist you in making parenting decisions that are more closely aligned with the needs of your child and your family, then the guidebook has achieved its secondary, deeper purpose. And, if you finish the activities in this guidebook and feel that the distance between you and your teenager has diminished to where connection is reestablished...then the author of this work will be ecstatic with joy!

This guidebook has been developed to help you to locate *them* in **their** current state. Only then can we make more informed decisions about parenting and responding to their new needs in this very vast, often tumultuous and deeply mysterious adult ocean.

~ Day 1 ~

"RED SKY IN THE MORNING"

Travelers of the sea used to share the saying "Red sky in morning, sailors take warning. Red sky at night, sailor's delight" to remind them of the signs to look for in anticipation of how the weather would unfold on the voyage. If you have a teenager at home, you definitely woke up to a red sky. The storm is, quite simply, change. No organism on this planet likes change. Change puts stress on any stable system. And in this case, the change is unavoidable, as it converts the child into the adult. So a storm is coming (or is already here), and there's nothing you can do to get out of the path. The best that we can do is to understand the course of the storm, and to respond effectively to the environment as it is impacted in the surge. And, we can't respond effectively if we aren't reading the signs accurately. The key here is to get to know the communication routes of our teenagers. It's not that we lose touch with them...but their methods are evolving into more complex ones than we have ever before seen displayed in our children. Think back to when your child was an infant. Each child has several different cries for different needs, right? There's the "my diaper needs to be changed" cry, which is different from the "I am hungry" cry, or even the "My tummy is upset and a big burp would bring relief right now" cry. And, you knew them all. Other people in the room hearing the same cry couldn't discern the repertoire. They may have even been other family members...aunts, uncles, siblings. It's not that they didn't care. It was the level of emotional intimacy and knowledge of subtle cues that indicated critical attributes of each and every cry. Learning those subtle nuances takes time...patience...and reflective effort. In the business of raising children and running a household, we lose track of time and the fact that our children are changing very, very rapidly during adolescence. We lose familiarity with the different cries. Now they are whines. Or temper tantrums. Sometimes the adolescent cry for attention and guidance is actually a silent withdrawal from routine. And, their logic, as we will discuss further in this section, has been sabotaged by other parts of their brain during adolescence. To further muddy the waters, we not only deal with times when we cannot read them accurately, but we realize that the goal we had in mind was very different from the goal our teenager had in mind. If we simply take the time to re-learn some of these new "cries" as parents, we can fully re-establish the connection with our teens. The calm, predictable waters of childhood are being replaced by a swift change in current. And whenever current directions and speeds change in the water, turmoil is inevitable. We know all-to-well that the adult world runs in a very rapid current with an even faster undertow. Our children have never seen such an unforgiving current. They are going to make mistakes. Their boat is going to capsize...again...and again...and again. There is no avoiding it, and the best chance of helping them to build their own navigation skills is not in avoiding the current...but providing a buoy...a safe haven to catch a breath. How do you, as a parent, know where to throw the buoy if you don't know where your child is in the water? How are we to pick up on the signal of a silent cry? We can, if we know what we are looking for.

Many of the behaviors teenagers display now seem absolutely counter-productive to the goals at hand. As parents, we use our best logic in attempting to sort out the rational thoughts behind their behaviors. And that is actually where we start to go off track in reading them. Teenagers are not being rational much of the time; they're being emotional. Let's look at two examples of questions that almost every parent asks their teenager after a perplexing behavior. "What were you thinking?!?" and "Why can't you just act your age?" I can even visualize my father's facial expression every time he posed those questions to me when I was on the receiving end. It was a combined look of "What on Earth is wrong with you?" and "Are you really my child? ...because I cannot wrap my head around your rationale for what you just said or did!"

The answer to the initial question is...that they aren't thinking. At least, not in the way adults do. And for the second question, they **are** acting their age. Let's go back and correct some of the misinformation we were given in school. At the time, it was the best information our science teachers had to offer, but the discoveries in science change every day. And numerous updates are directly related to how we understand the human brain. Many of us were told that you are born with all of your neurons already present and connected to each other at birth. We now know that the brain continues to develop neurons far beyond birth. And the connections between neurons are still being shaped even into your early twenties! When we are born, less than 20% of our neurons are actually linked to each other. In fact, adolescence is a time of what is called "blossoming", when neurons are rapidly connecting to each other, especially in the pre-frontal cortex, where problem-solving skills and reasoning functions are located. In fact, the neurons are growing so fast in this region...(the peak development for this region is ages 11 to 12) that they aren't really fully engaged and "online" yet (Giedd, 2012). What IS online, unfortunately, is the limbic system (located in the center of the brain), which is the center of our emotions.

The limbic system includes structures called the amygdala and the hippocampus. The amygdala is the center for "fight or flight" as well as the basis of fear and anger. This is a region that triggers survival instincts. It is designed to override logic, which could take too long to process answers in a life-threatening situation. The hippocampus is responsible for encoding new memories...such as initial learning. It also regulates emotional connections (the formation of relationships) to other individuals. Both of these structures are highly active in teenagers of either gender. In terms of gender, the amygdala is very sensitive to the increases of testosterone that boys encounter during adolescence. Conversely, the hippocampus in a girl has more receptors for growth and development hormones (like estrogen and progesterone) than a boy's brain. Another interesting difference is in the process of myelination, which is when the axons of many neurons develop a type of "insulation" that will make neural connections faster and more efficient. The neurons in female teenagers myelinate at a faster rate than those in a male teen. This can explain some of the fine motor skills that are more advanced in females than in males in high school. By the end of adolescence, though, the two genders have caught-up in this category (Walsh, 2004). At this point, some of the gender differences that we see in the **behaviors** during the teen years may be making more sense as well. It is because of these hormonal differences that many researchers think we sometimes see an accentuation in many male teens who display impulse issues; while some female teens have a heightened sensitivity to the formation of relationships and changes in the dynamics of those bonds.

Another interesting finding by Dr. Deborah Yurgelin-Todd is that teenagers have difficulty accurately identifying the emotions displayed in adult facial expressions. For example, they may read an expression as anger that is really showing fear or concern. Does this sound familiar? Again, this is the limbic system in hyper-drive. At the same time, the pre-frontal cortex has not yet matured to temper and filter the emotional responses or to bring a logical application to what the teenager is experiencing. The list below is a compilation of typical behaviors in teenagers. See if some of these look familiar in your situation:

- Different child at school than at home
- Very hard to wake up in the morning
- Staying up late into the night
- Forgetful when asked to do things
- Talk before they think...verbally impulsive
- Self-absorbed and near-sighted about goals
- Moody, anxious and easily agitated
- Unpredictable with mood changes...very mercurial
- Physically awkward
- Argumentative...sometimes to the point of counter productivity
- Overwhelmed by little things...loss of perspective
- Can't discern "big issues" from "little issues"...prioritization issues
- Insecure...taking everything personally
- Very emotionally expressive...lacking salience with the situation at hand

If you found that even half of these describe your teenager (or all of them), know that you are **not** alone. In fact, you are in the majority. And, all of these characteristics are normal. This means that as a parent trying to find the calm in the storm, the two best skills for us to possess, not only in trying to maintain our own sanity, but also in trying to successfully deal with and guide our adolescents, is to be **flexible to change** and to **improve our communication skills** when trying to read their current state.

Another major factor to keep in mind is that the neurons that have been going through a rapid period of "blossoming" will later go through a period called "pruning". This is when the brain trims back and reduces those neurons that are not being used. Thus, many researchers are now concerned with (and studying) the effects that excessive hours playing video games rather than interacting socially and building communication skills may have on the adolescent brain (Giedd, 2012).

Before we really begin this 30 day voyage, it might be helpful to reflect on the big picture. Where have they been as infants and children, where are our teenagers right now, and where are they going? Erik Erikson was one of the founding researchers in developmental psychology. He spent the majority of his life studying the interrelationships of how the individual develops not only within himself, but socially interacting with others. He is the psychologist who created the term "identity crisis", which is really what your child is going through right now (and perhaps, you too, as a result). For the first year of life, we learn to either trust or distrust our caregivers for the physical and psychological essentials we need to survive. In our toddler years, we develop a sense of autonomy or it reverts to shame and doubt about our own abilities to navigate our immediate realities and to predict the environment around us. The preschool stage involves initiative versus guilt whereby we discover a sense of accomplishment. At six to eleven years of age, humans learn which tasks they can do for themselves (such as dressing ourselves, solving basic problems, and how our abilities compare to those of other children. This is sometimes called the industry – inferiority stage. "I can do it myself!" But look out now!

From ages 12-18, we experience a time of identity versus role confusion. We begin to question ourselves and how we fit in with others and the big social picture. We try on other roles, those of our parents, teachers, and peers. At many times, we don't like who we are. And most of the time, we simply don't know who we are. This is a time of wandering and searching. You know this phase well. Right now it probably feels like being stuck in a bed of oozing mud that is aflame with hot coals that seem to extend in every direction with no end in sight. Oh wait, that would be hell. And yes, you're in it. You'd have to read Dante's *Inferno* to figure out which ring you have descended to in this storm of adolescence. I'm guessing it's pretty deep.

Just when you thought it couldn't get more fun than this, somewhere in the mid-teenage years through to roughly the late twenties comes the stage of intimacy versus isolation. This is when we extend ourselves to love another. If we are having difficulty forming and maintaining those bonds, we become isolated and alone. There are two other stages to Erikson's theory, but we will leave those for guides addressing the mid-life crisis and growing old...two stages we are all looking forward to in the years to come. Below are two columns showing some descriptions of the individual in the identity versus role confusion stage combined with characteristics of the intimacy versus isolation stage. Take a few minutes to look at this list, and check mark those that apply to your adolescent as more of an "either-or" for each row across the two columns. This will give you a rough idea of where your teen is in the process. However, as you have probably already observed, these phases of psychology are never directly linear. They are rife with starts and stops, some lasting longer than others with no regularity of time, and in many cases, humans even back-track or loop around to revisit a previous stage. It's like we haven't quite finished one task when we jump into the next one. Adolescence is not simple. People are not simple. When viewing the lists below, think of the descriptions that are across from each other as more of a "continuum" rather than an "either-or" situation.

Heading Into the Storm

- Seek self-acceptance by being what others want them to be

- Unstable self-concept with many ups and downs

- Have trouble making decisions

- Develop competitive relationships, making cooperation difficult

- Tend to prefer separation from others

- Perceive that relationships are for "taking", not sharing together

- Cynical about self, others, and life

- Sex is perceived as a means of physical satisfaction, partner is an object

- Have difficulty expressing and verbalizing feelings

- Very susceptible to peer pressure influences

- Not tolerant or accepting of differences in other people

- Inflexible and insist that they are right

- Difficulty establishing long-term goals

- Many periods of low self-acceptance

Coming Out of the Storm

- Self-acceptance doesn't rest within opinions of others

- Self-concept is more stable and not changed by situations

- Decisions are easily made without wavering

- Relationships are more cooperative now

- Find satisfaction in being part of a group

- Relationships are when you give and share

- Optimistic about self, others, and life

- Sex is about physical closeness AND communicating love

- Able to express feelings of care without fear

- Peer influences do not alter core personality

- More tolerant and accepting of differences in others

- Being right is not ego driven but based on facts

- Able to accomplish long-term goals

- Self-acceptance is present and stable

ASSESSING THE STORM

Of all the characteristics listed on the previous page, there are probably several that you indicated as ones found in your own teenager. Many times when we try to alter too many behavioral responses in someone, we end up compromising the entire effort. The person feels overwhelmed, picked-upon, as if they can't do anything right. The activity for this first day is to select only three of the behaviors that affect the calm dynamics of your family the most. Throughout the 30 day guidebook timeline, try to focus only on these three specific behaviors to address in your child's personality at this time. Many of the days and activities that follow will come back to this "list of three".

In addition to limiting the majority of our efforts on this work, it's also beneficial to take a moment and reflect on three qualities we see in our children that are absolutely unique to themselves (not directly from either parent) and that not only compliment their personality, but also enhance the lives of people around them. This will helps us to focus on positive qualities while we are dealing with the variables that make the storms so rough. And, these positive qualities will most likely be present...and even more wonderfully developed...in the adult that will eventually emerge and occupy a different niche in the family.

Three Characteristics to Improve: **Three Strength Characteristics:**

_____   _____

_____   _____

_____   _____

~ Day 2 ~

STURM UND DRANG

No, the author didn't just switch languages on you. "Sturm und drang" is an expression originating in the 1700s that describes movements in literature and music that were designed to lead the audience into extremes of emotion. It translates to "storm and stress". No part of the ship is going to encounter greater effects of life's storms than the hull of the ship. And the hull is not only what keeps the ship afloat. In the world of psychology, what keeps our emotional state afloat is, in part, resilience. So, to begin our journey, what we need are two assessments. The first one will address the severity of the storms that your child is encountering during adolescence. This instrument will assess the levels of stress both you and your teenager are feeling at this time. The second instrument is one that will measure the strength of the hull, which is actually an assessment of a person's coping mechanisms.

Stress has always had a very strange relationship with motivation. Even if we go back to a single-celled organism like an amoeba, stress is what causes changes. If the amoeba senses a decrease in water volume, it will attempt adjustments to take-on more water through osmosis across the membrane. If the environment doesn't have enough water, the amoeba may die. If it happens to be an amoeba with cilia (little hair structures on the cell membrane), it can move around a bit in the environment...perhaps even to another area that does have enough moisture. Then, it will live another day. As much as we would like to think that we are substantially different from these little creatures...in fact, we are not. At least, this is not in the sense of responding to stress. Granted, we are multicellular and have numerous complete body systems. That basically means that we have many parts of our bodies that can encounter different types and degrees of stress. And, we have numerous ways to deal with and try to reduce the stress, which is not a luxury afforded to the amoeba. It's life is very simple and immediate. So is its response to stress and the results of that response. Sometimes for us, the stresses we encounter have many variables that led to the stress. And given that we have a very complex nervous system complete with limbic structures that bring with them an entire palate of emotional response, not all of our stresses are physical. In fact, many psychologists would argue that most of our stresses are emotionally induced. (Sapolsky, 1998)

There is no question that, as the loving and dedicated parent(s) of an adolescent, you are stressed. If you weren't, you wouldn't have searched for this guidebook. And it is by no means an indication of insignificance of your stress level that we are going to spend very little time in the introductory chapters on your stress as opposed to that of your child. But given that much of your stress is in response to your child, let's get to the core matter rather than just the symptom response. It is my hope that, during the course of 30 days of working through this guidebook, you will begin to feel your stress abate as you observe the same in your child. Many of the activities found in this guidebook are meant to bring a greater sense of calm and reassurance to the entire family of an adolescent.

Believe it or not, stress can be your ally **IF** it is the right kind of stress in the right amount and lasts for a limited duration. Stress is simply movement away from homeostasis, or balance, in your body systems. Even if your body is only composed of one cell (amoebas are now excited to be included in this guidebook), when you encounter *anything* that moves you from balance, stress is encountered. For amoebas, this might be a decrease in water volume, or an increase in temperature, or a change in atmospheric pressure. For those of us who are more complex than amoebas, there are numerous systems that are all interconnected and continuously affecting each other. Thus, a decrease in water volume (if it is great enough) can effect numerous systems and display stress via multiple responses that can be detected through changes in vital signs, volume of urine output, amount of sweat produced, etc. The amazing thing is that, some organisms have even evolved further and possess a limbic system that carries emotional responses to situations in addition to physical responses. The types of stress we encounter are not just physiological, but also psychological.   And, the psychological stressors can affect the physiological homeostasis!

With layers of research to support the findings, it is now very clear that stress can compromise our immune systems in both short-term and long-term ways. As a teacher, it is not uncommon to see the legitimate illnesses encountered by high school students increasing just before final exams or just after the testing period. Some students have response systems that can "hold it together" until the tests are over...and then crash. Others can't hold out that long. And for still others, we see (thankfully) an adaptive ability to handle these emotional stressors in a manner that allows them to continue their higher performance levels on final exams. I wish I could tell you exactly what those differences are in each of my students, but that is the next layer (and decade) of research that is being conducted as you read this sentence. While we know the metabolic triggers and routes of stress now (levels of cortisol, neurotransmitters that respond to stress, etc.), the connection points at the cellular and subcellular level that are still being deduced. And now we are even aware of the epigenetic factors that alter the expression of our genes. Some people are predisposed to be very sensitive to stressors, while others are not; just as some people are very sensitive to changes in motion and others are not.

Epigenetics (basically, whether your genes are "turned-on" or "turned-off") can, in part, explain how some people carry genetic markers for certain environmental responses, diseases, allergies, etc. and express the trait; while other individuals who carry the exact same genetic marker do not express the same trait. There are numerous cases of identical twins carrying the same genetic marker for certain diseases, but only one twin actually develops the disease. In many of these cases, it has been discovered that the gene for the disease has been switched on or off in one of the siblings, resulting in a difference of outcome.   There are many different environmental factors (such as pollutants, hormones, drugs, radiation, etc.) that can sometimes switch genes "on" and "off". Even dietary conditions such as famines have actually been found to have an epigenetic effect on the individuals who survived the event as well as all of their descendants (Heijmans, 2008). A very controversial but consistently supported finding revealed that even the genes and cortisol levels in babies born of women who were pregnant and present during the 9-11 attacks of the World Trade Center were affected (Yehuda, 2005). The magnitude of this is almost beyond comprehension. Factors that affected the quality of life in your great, great grandparents can be present in your genes and have an effect in your life. And, the factors you encounter can affect great, great grandchildren that you will never directly meet. The ripple effects of what we do, what we eat, and the environments we encounter in our lives actually transcend time.

Is your child's response to stress and anxiety partly genetic / inherited? Yes...partly. And part of his or her response is also learned. The answer is a mixture of factors and percents that are yet unknown. Even then, the percents of different sources for these traits may not be the same for every person. In other words, my response to emotional stress may be 60% inherited, while yours is only 40% inherited. And, I have learned different methods of displaying and coping with my stress than you did in your upbringing, school history, and influences of friends, etc. Researchers have also concluded that high levels of stress "short circuit" or override our pre-frontal cortex, which is where higher order thinking and problem-solving occur. Add this to the fact that for humans, our limbic system matures at a faster rate than our pre-frontal cortex. If we go back a few million years ago, this would have served us well in a different environment. As we went through puberty, the impulsiveness and risk-taking that are, in today's world, so problematic for teens, would have actually saved them from situations in which their lives were at risk as they ventured out beyond the safety circle of their parents and into unfamiliar and unfiltered territory. They would have been quick to respond, and willing to try anything. If a carnivore was chasing a newly-emerged adult, there would be a higher chance of finding a solution and going with it. "Climbing that tree not only looks good, I'm already there!" Change the setting, and we now have a very fast-paced environment with technology that puts both advantage...and harm...within arm's reach. "Flooring the accelerator to see what happens" suddenly introduces a very high risk of injury or death as opposed to saving us from a carnivore. Sapolsky describes the attributes of **good** stress that directs us toward positive change as having three basic qualities. Good stress is moderate; not too much and (believe it or not) not too little tends to generate the greatest productivity. If a child is not stressed at all, they will not study, take out the trash, clean their bedroom, or change negative behaviors. If they are overly stressed, they tend to shut down and lose productivity entirely. Second, good stress is short-term in duration. If a child is under stress for a lengthy period, they can either move into a perception of increased levels of stress, or extinction (in which they lose responsiveness). And third, the context in which the stressor occurs is predictable (Sapolsky, 1989).

Providing a known context or environment allows for control of personal response and a clear awareness of the desired outcome. Once the rules or the setting changes abruptly or unpredictably, all bets are off. And, the child is likely to lose motivation. For example, if a child does not feel some stress to clean his or her room, they never will. If they do not understand what "clean" means to the parent (or if details are added after-the-fact), then the contextual rules have been altered. A typical verbal response to this break in the context might be, "Well then, just forget it." Or, "There's no way I can win with you!" There is a haunting truth in this last sentence. The child can't "win" or accomplish the task because the target goal keeps moving. There is a big difference in asking a child to clean his/her room "now" when this activity was unexpected throughout the day prior to the exchange between parent and child, versus saying "Please have your room clean by dinner time at 6:00." Now the child has predictability, and has even retained the decision of exactly *when* the task will be completed. Perhaps the stress to clean her room comes in the form of frustration when she is unable to find her cell phone under the bed, or it may come from an ultimatum offered by the parent...such as, "You may not go out with your friends *until* your room is clean."

Knowing your child and which motivators induce a moderate amount of stress for that particular individual are critical to success when trying to accomplish goals. In addition, stress inducers vary with circumstances and development. When my own child was five, the stressor to clean the room was the example given above as a specific time for completion. As a teenager, it was the "key" to being able to leave the house to socialize with peers. Now that he is in his twenties and in his own apartment, the stressor is an impending visit from his girlfriend. Nice. (And sometimes as a parent, even though the outcome is one you desired, you're not really sure if you appreciate the means to the goal...)

When children do homework, we often see different inducers as well...avoidance of getting grounded, maintaining a certain grade, and hopefully...for the inherent value of understanding the material. (Which can cyclically lead back to good grades and not getting grounded!) Of course, what works for one child does not always work for another child. In fact, those parents with more than one child will frequently attest to that. Teachers see this in the form of comments during conferences like, "I just don't understand. All I had to do with my oldest child was remind her of the test on Friday, and she would do her homework immediately. My youngest has no concern what-so-ever about the upcoming test...and we have to remove his video game privileges much of the time. And THAT doesn't even work in some cases." Right. Different children. Different motivators. Some individuals are intrinsically motivated; factors within the individual are driving the person to achieve. And others are extrinsically motivated, with factors in the environment providing the push to accomplish goals. In fact, temporally and psychologically speaking, the two children weren't even raised by the same parents.

Now that we understand some of the aspects of how stress affects not only our health, but the interactions of our relationships, let's look at a stress scale that actually quantifies the level of stress from life-changing events that we could encounter over the course of any given year. The original Holmes-Rahe Stress Inventory was developed in 1967 by two psychiatrists who assessed over 5,000 patients, all adults. What they discovered was a significant positive correlation between stress levels and actual medical illnesses. These studies were replicated numerous times with consistently supportive outcomes over the decades.

However, teenagers will have different stressors than parents, and vice-versa. So modifications to the original list of stressors were developed and tested that would specifically address adolescents. The task for today is to look at the Stress Inventory that spans the next several pages and note the stressors listed while thinking about the experiences of your own child. Then, quantify the total stress level that **you** perceive for your child. Next, give the inventory to your child (without seeing your results) and then compare the two outcomes...yours and your child's. Not only is it very valuable to actually see the numbers and types of stressors generated by each person (parent and child), but to then assess how accurate you were in being an outside observer of your child's life.

Remember that perception is everything. Your child's score of his/her own life is actually more valid than your assessment. The closer your scores are to each other, the more aware and "in-tune" you are with how your child perceives their reality. There are many versions of the Holmes-Rahe in the public today. This author specifically analyzed and compiled the one seen here from four different sources: one version created for younger children, one for adolescents, one for college students, and the original inventory. Thus, you will see ranges on some categories as these will vary based on the stage of development and the variables influencing the stressor and the teenager's perception of events.

After your teen completes the Teen Stress Inventory, consider sharing a few memories from your adolescence that generated a lot of stress for you, and which productive strategies you learned and used to deal with the situation.

TEEN STRESS INVENTORY

This inventory is a compilation of several different versions for ages pre-teen through college, with adjustments from later researchers and this author modifying the stressors to align with those encountered by teenagers in our society. Remember that this is a perception inventory. There are no absolute truths that can be applied from one situation to another, or one family to another. The validity of this activity is in what it reveals and how it strengthens the communication and understanding between you and your teenager.

Check all of the items that you have dealt with in the past 12 months. When you finish, add up all the points of the changes you have experienced. Where ranges are provided, select the exact number that you perceive as reflecting your level of stress for that event. For example, there is a range on "Breakup with boyfriend/girlfriend" as more stress may be encountered if one member of the relationship did not expect or want the breakup as opposed to the other individual feeling the breakup was necessary and thus, the action was predicted. The same is true for the range on "Parent remarries" based on how the child perceives the new relationship and step-parent as a positive or negative change in family dynamics.

Stressor	Point Value
Death of a parent	100
Parents divorced	75
Unwed pregnancy	65-90
Father of unwed pregnancy	77
Change in acceptance by peers	67
Parents separated	65
Close family member died	60-68
Breakup with boyfriend/girlfriend	40-60
Death of a close friend	40-60
Failure of a grade in school	56
Not making an extracurricular activity	55
Serious personal illness or injury	45-50

_____	Increase in arguments with parents	45
_____	Parent loses job	46
_____	Entering middle school/high school/college 1st year	45
_____	Habitual drug or alcohol abuse	45-70
_____	Parent remarried	35-60
_____	Birth of a brother or sister	35-50
_____	Being a senior with college selections	43
_____	Trouble at school	40
_____	Confusion of sexual identity	35
_____	Work while attending school	35
_____	Outstanding personal achievement/award	25-35
_____	Older sibling left home	29-37
_____	Moved to another part of town or city	26
_____	Sleeping less than 8 hours a night	25
_____	Change in living conditions (location)	20
_____	Presently in, and affected by, pre-menstrual part of cycle	15
_____	Presently in Winter holiday season or Spring break	10

_____	**TOTAL** from the list of stressors	

0	-	149	Relatively low and manageable stresses
150	-	200	Slightly increased risk of stress-induced illness
200	-	299	Moderately increased risk of stress-related illness
300	-	Higher	Major stress exists - very high possibility of illness

INTERPRETIVE PERSPECTIVES FOR PARENTS:

An initial reminder that any type of change causes stress to a person, whether it is perceived as "good" or "bad". This can be seen in stressors such as holiday breaks from school when teenagers are not near their friends and are temporarily removed from the routine of school that keeps them synchronized. Or when considering changes in living conditions, whether due to financial strain into a smaller dwelling or increased income resulting in a bigger house, these variables will also manifest in the results. In addition, a person's perspective is their own and holds validity without any need for justification. If your child feels that the birth of a new sibling was a "42" and you feel it should be a "43"...it's a 42 for your child. If your teenager is asked to "defend" any of these numbers, it will not only defeat the purpose of the inventory as it is applied within this guidebook, but will negatively impact your communication with your child from this point throughout the 30 day process!

Parents will also observe that this scale is based on teenagers and their view of the world. In the inventory, it actually rates "change in acceptance by peers" higher in stress than "failing a grade". Knowing the long-term effects of a failing grade, a parent would likely perceive that this should be rated far higher than a mere change in peer acceptance. However, peer acceptance at the age of 40 is not nearly as important as it is at age 14. And, a teenager's life is centered around their peers and social circle. Thus, more variables are "pinned" or connected to the shifts in peers than would be encountered with changes in friends as a full adult. In addition, we need to keep in mind that a teenager of 13 will have very different perceptions of these categories compared to one who is 18. And, unfortunately, a teenager will not fully understand the future implications of those grades until they are actually living in the future. The same was true for us. If your children could osmotically absorb your view of life and these issues, you wouldn't need this guidebook.

Not only is age within the adolescent years a significant variable, but any factors that are tied to these categories can actually amplify the resulting stress felt by the individual.

This is similar to "comorbidity" in medicine and psychology whereby one trait (or illness in those cases) actually affects the other. Another factor is initial onset versus time to adjust. For example, if a parent remarries, the level of stress will be very different on the week of the actual wedding ceremony and "moving-in together" versus six months later...even though both occur within the same year. A teen who is very stressed in September could be mildly stressed in November.

Now that we know our stress number, it is important to be aware of some of the effects of stress. Cognitively, stress blocks access to memory, which means it is hard to study as well as hard to recall information during a test if a student is highly stressed beyond a moderate range. Also, stress affects decision-making skills and decreases our ability to focus attention. In terms of emotions, anxiety increases, the little things tend to push us beyond threshold more readily, and in extreme or prolonged cases, depression and anger issues can result. When we are under high levels of stress, we also exhibit changes in behaviors like eating, sleeping (a marked increase or decrease), procrastinating, development of nervous habits (nail biting, hair-pulling, etc.), and a decrease or even complete isolation in peer interactions. Thus, checking-in and taking this survey from time-to-time in the future could also help a person's awareness as circumstances change.

With these added variables in mind, what is more important to this author is **NOT** the actual rating numbers, but where they sit contextually in comparison to other stressors on the list. Focusing on this perspective allows us to observe and feel our child's world from their viewpoint. It also reminds us of some stressors that are much greater in these early years than they are once we are adults. Your child may have indicated that the breakup of a romantic relationship was at a "60", when you might be feeling, "That kid was a jerk, anyway. My child is better off without that influence." You are relieved. Your child is devastated. It's important to return to *their* viewpoint. This is a major relationship for teenagers. They have never been twenty or thirty-something...yet. That requires a lot of growth in the heart, not just the body. They don't the feeling of how love deepens with maturity, and that the love of marriage is much deeper than dating couples. They've never been married yet. Conversely, they've never gone through a divorce. If a parent is currently going through the dissolution of a marriage, it is sometimes hard to sympathize fully with our teenager who is going through a breakup. Believe it or not, their pain can be as great as yours, it's just a very different scale. A smaller heart breaks more easily. And to accent the emotional stress of the experiences they are going through compared to those of an adult, they do not yet have the support of knowing that they can and will pull through these rough storms. Nor do they have the array of coping mechanisms that adults have, hopefully, fully developed and employed in many circumstances. Time is not yet on their side. After a person has been through a dozen break-ups, he/she is more certain that their heart can mend and that it really isn't the end of the world.

Consider describing to your teenager a time when you had a major change in stability in your life (perhaps a reconfiguration of the family, moving to another city, or the birth of a new sibling), or perhaps even a broken heart. But as you describe the event, include how it FELT and not just the physical details of the memory.

Relationships:

Parents

The relationship that teens have with their parents is one that changes as the boundaries of their lives begin to rapidly expand on all horizons. The parents, in part, are viewed as the "safe port" when weathering storms. They are the base of communication...not only between generations within a family, but also the translation point between the environment and members of the family. Home is where you re-stock your supplies. That means that parents are seen as a source of support, encouragement, renewal of energy, and tangible resources. As parents, it is important to remember that, eventually, we want these "baby birds" to leave the nest. And this process does not occur overnight. It begins slowly with their cognitive and emotional development into adulthood...and ends somewhere between "can you help me with a down payment on the house" and "what should we do if the baby has a fever?" Many would argue that it is never a complete severing...but more a redefining of needs and wants.

From a teacher's perspective, this is a period of time when conflict is building from the pre-teen years and throughout college life. And, this conflict is NOT a reflection on your parenting skills, intellectual abilities, nor your devotion level with your child. Rather, it is about a young adult trying to define him/herself. "How am I similar to my parents...and how am I different?" "What parts of 'me' are just 'me'?"

~ Day 3 ~

LOADING SUPPLIES FROM THE DOCK

It is imperative that we take a careful inventory of the supplies aboard our ship before departing from the dock. Anything we require will, of course, need to be with us on the journey. Sometimes this causes a great deal of anxiety in the parents of teenage children as they think ahead and realize that you can almost count the days until they are living on their own and will want a good stock of supplies. We lose a great deal of sleep thinking about questions like, "What will she do if she gets too stressed-out on campus?" or "What if she ends up marrying someone who isn't good for her?" The list of concerns can go on forever. But one of the greatest tools to have onboard one's personality is that of resilience. It is one of the first traits we resort to when we encounter social and emotional obstacles.

Resilience is the ability a person has to handle stress and overcome adversity to achieve positive developmental outcomes. Resilience is the characteristic or trait, while coping is the action or strategy. The good news is that, while some people innately have more resilience than others, it is a trait that can be learned and developed in a person as it is not solely based on genetic factors, but also many environmental components (Goldstein, 2006). The American Psychological Association lists several factors that contribute to building resilience including the following:

- making connections with others
- accepting that change is a natural part of life
- movement toward personal goals
- nurturing a positive view of oneself
- maintaining a hopeful outlook on situations
- looking for opportunities of self-discovery and personal growth
- avoid seeing crises as being insurmountable
- taking decisive action

Concern arises when teenagers, who are already struggling with self-identity and personal empowerment issues, do not have the resources or opportunities to develop these skills. For example, the CDC reports that 30% of teenage suicides are connected to alcohol or drug use, and that half of all adolescent vehicle accidents are associated with the same two variables (2002). Alcohol and drug use are coping strategies (maladaptive ones) for individuals who do not have or use positive coping mechanisms. Their resilience threshold is lower in these individuals, leading to a faster response including the selection of maladaptive coping strategies (DeVore, 2005).

Another factor associated with displaying resilience during times of stress is parenting style (which we will cover in the next chapter). And, the parenting style most associated with the development of resilience in our children is the authoritative style (Goldstein, 2006). This method focuses on building the child's sense of self-competence, unconditional love and acceptance not contingent on behaviors, and contributing to the daily functions of the family unit. Now, we will turn our efforts toward identifying those coping strategies that are currently used by our teenagers. Some of these are innately favored, others are learned in their environment, and many developed as a combination of both. But once we know which strategies we use, then we can determine if they are ones that lead us to positive, personal growth outcomes, or negative, maladaptive ones that derail our growth and ability to achieve our goals. The activity today is taking an assessment of coping strategies, for both you and your teenager.

The Teen Coping Inventory

Respond to each of the items by writing a number beside each description (use the guide below) in the answer sheet provided. Try to respond to each item separately from the other ones presented. There are no "right" or "wrong" answers, so choose the one that is best for YOU...not what you think "most people" would say or do.

Once you have finished all 30 items, transcribe your answers to the analysis sheet. Answer these as they would apply when you are dealing with an issue that has elevated your stress level considerably.

1 = "I don't do this at all."
2 = "I usually don't do this."
3 = "I sometimes do this."
4 = "I almost always do this."

1. I try to grow as a result of the experience and learn from it.
2. I go to movies, play video games, or watch TV to think about it less.
3. I get upset about it and let my emotions out.
4. I try to get advice from someone about what to do.
5. I concentrate my efforts on doing something about the issue.
6. I pretend that the issue hasn't really happened.
7. I put my trust in a higher power to get me through.
8. I kid around about my problems and the amount of stress I have.
9. I admit to myself that I can't deal with it; and quit trying 'cause there's no point.
10. I try to avoid making matters worse by acting too soon.
11. I discuss my feelings with someone who will sympathize with me.
12. I use alcohol or other drugs to make myself feel better and get me through.
13. I get used to the idea that it happened and just get used to it.
14. I ask other people who have gone through the same stuff what they did.
15. I keep myself from getting distracted by other thoughts / activities until I solve it.
16. I sleep more than usual because of the stress.
17. I feel really emotionally stressed-out and express those feelings a lot.
18. I rely on my religion or beliefs to understand the issue.
19. I think about the best way for me to handle the problem and make a plan.

20. I make jokes about the issue even though it's not funny.
21. I accept that this has happened and that it can't be changed.
22. I hold off doing anything about it until the situation permits.
23. I try to get emotional support from friends or relatives.
24. I just give up trying to reach my goal and accomplish things.
25. I take action to try to solve the problem.
26. I try to lose myself for a while by drinking alcohol or taking drugs.
27. I refuse to believe that it has happened.
28. I think hard about what steps to take to solve the problem.
29. I try to see it in a different light, to make it seem more positive.
30. I focus on dealing with this problem, and if necessary let other things slide a little.

<u>Analysis of the Teen Coping Inventory:</u>

1. _____	11. _____	21. _____
2. _____	12. _____	22. _____
3. _____	13. _____	23. _____
4. _____	14. _____	24. _____
5. _____	15. _____	25. _____
6. _____	16. _____	26. _____
7. _____	17. _____	27. _____
8. _____	18. _____	28. _____
9. _____	19. _____	29. _____
10. _____	20. _____	30. _____

Transcribe your answers by number into each category:

Positive interpretation & growth: 1: _____ 29: _____   Total: _____

Mental disengagement: 2: _____ 16: _____   Total: _____

Focus on and venting of emotions: 3: _____ 17: _____   Total: _____

Use of positive social support: 4: _____ 14: _____   Total: _____

Active coping: 5: _____ 25: _____   Total: _____

Denial: 6: _____ 27: _____   Total: _____

Religious coping: 7: _____ 18: _____   Total: _____

Humor: 8: _____ 20: _____   Total: _____

Behavioral disengagement: 9: _____ 24: _____   Total: _____

Restraint: 10: _____ 22: _____   Total: _____

Use of emotional social support: 11: _____ 23: _____   Total: _____

Substance use: 12: _____ 26: _____   Total: _____

Acceptance: 13: _____ 21: _____   Total: _____

Suppression of competing activities: 15: _____ 30: _____   Total: _____

Planning: 19: _____ 28: _____   Total: _____

NOTES OF ANY TRENDS:

SOURCE:

Carver, C. S., Scheier, M. F., & Weintraub, J. K. (1989). Assessing coping strategies: A theoretically based approach. *Journal of Personality and Social Psychology*, 56, 267-283.

INTERPRETING RESULTS FROM THE TEEN COPING SKILLS INVENTORY

Remember that this information is just that...information. It is not a diagnosis, nor a prognosis. The scores are neither "good" nor "bad" in any of the above categories. They simply clarify how an individual copes with stress. And, we all encounter stress. We all have different coping mechanisms. If we didn't have these mechanisms, the stress would affect us in very adverse ways. Some of the areas that people use to help them deal with emotions, however, may be maladaptive over a period of or when contextually applied in certain situations time (i.e. substance abuse, denial, mental disengagement). Recall that the context and the reason for using various coping strategies are part of determining whether they are effective or not. For example, mental disengagement in the form of **temporarily** going to a movie or working in the garage on a hobby (numbers 2 and 16 on the inventory) so that we avoid an escalation in a conflict (and perhaps saying something that we will later regret). This also allows many people time to reflect and provide an opportunity for our problem-solving regions of the brain to regain perspective from our emotional limbic system may, in the long run, be quite productive toward achieving the overall goal of returning to a constructive discussion that brings about resolution. Using these same mechanisms every time there is a verbal altercation with parents and **not** returning to the issue for resolution at a later time can be very detrimental for all parties involved. An individual can use this information to assess their general direction and productivity levels in life. If desired, they can access further information to alter their own behaviors into more positive patterns with beneficial outcomes.

~ Day 4 ~

ANCHORS AWAY!

What? Yes...consider that as parents for the first time, you were very different in your thoughts, actions, and parental approaches with the oldest child compared to the second child, or third, etc. Remember the old Chinese proverb, "You can never step in the same river twice"? You aren't the same person you were yesterday. Of course, yesterday was only 24 hours ago, and the number of experiences you have had in that short time have been fairly limited. So, the difference between the "yesterday you" and the "today you" are very small. But extend that amount of time to many years and many experiences, and the differences just increase exponentially. Now take another look at your children and the parents THEY observed during the same age...say at five years old. Different, right? In part, this is why so many findings about birth order hold validity. There are *some* similarities in almost all new parents. They are all...very, very nervous. And their first-born knows it. And the child naturally responds to it. The second child will not observe nearly as much nervousness in the parents as the first child did. Hence, a different outcome in the developing personality of the second child, as well. And so on. Also consider those changes that are more radical, such as changes in jobs, geography, extended family relationships, etc. Consider the following scenarios:

Child A is a first-born with parents who are still finishing their college degrees. There's not much money to be spared. Clothing is limited and usually comes from hand-me-downs from an older cousin. Late nights are spent studying. The parents are exhausted with trying to hold down both jobs and school work. But, both parents are very young and very passionate...about life, their careers, and each other.

Child B is the second-born with parents who are both professionals holding graduate degrees. Money is not an issue...in fact, there are many family trips to various places with lots of experiences. Perhaps this child is a different gender than the oldest...with few, or no, hand-me-downs. Since money is not an issue, most clothes are brand new...and very trendy. Parents have more time to spend at home in the evenings with the children and each other.

Child C is the last born with parents who are struggling to keep a marriage going in which differences have started to show damage in the relationship. In response to the stresses, one parent is frequently not at home. The other might be compensating and spending a great deal of time with this child. Or perhaps a divorce is imminent, and the parent wanting to be with the youngest child has to find a second job to make ends meet. The oldest child is occupied with adolescence. The middle child is dealing with abrupt changes from "what was" to "what is now" regarding family dynamics. Everyone in the family is distracted and going in different directions for different reasons.

It doesn't take much description of their backgrounds to see that each of these children will, in time, recall a very different childhood from the other siblings. It's like they grew up in three different families. In some respects, they did. Many of the findings about trends in family constellations (such as being first-born, middle child, or a twin, etc.) are studied by numerous psychologists and researchers. From my perspective, the one who pioneered these studies and drew the patterns into a very cohesive understanding for both educators and parents was Dr. Kevin Leman. His original work in the field covers everything from gender differences in siblings, step-family configurations, and even birth order combinations in marriages (Leman, 2009).

Teachers can easily spot the "oldest child" of many families within the classroom. The same is true for the "youngest child". Middle children are a little harder to spot, as there are many variables within that category, which is evident in the variance of behaviors in this group. Are you the middle of three? Eight? The only boy? Is the oldest child ten years older than you? This is reductionist, but the oldest children are typically the overachievers who are stressing themselves out because their "A" in your class is not quite high enough...for them. As a teacher, I've had to remind many of these kiddos that the learning and achievement increase indicated from ...say, a grade of 85% up to a 93% in just two weeks is astounding and to be commended. The youngest ones, bless their little hearts, are the ones that keep smiling as the grade drops from a "B" to a "C" with no rise in blood pressure on their part. Their parents, however, will compensate with quite an increase in blood pressure and emails...not understanding why they care more about the grade than this particular child does. Knowing this aspect of a student's background helps the teacher (and the parents at home) to assess which avenues of motivation might work best for the success of this particular child in the classroom.

Another key factor in how our children's personalities and communication styles are shaped is that of parenting style. One of the original core researchers to study and categorize characteristics in parenting, Diana Baumrind, defined the three major styles as authoritarian, permissive (indulgent or indifferent), and authoritative types. For the activity today, view the descriptions of each parenting style listed below, and identify which one is most accurate to your family structure. But before you do this, know that most parents, when asked, think that they are authoritative. And actually, most are not. Try to be as objective as possible. When in doubt (I *think* I'm this way...but am I really?), know that most parents tend to parent in the same style in which their parents functioned. Think back to your own childhood and what you observed. While you may have shifted on the continuum of behaviors ("My father was really strict. I'm not nearly as strict as he was!") you are probably closer to their responses then you realize. Your observation may be true in relation to your father, but are you more strict than an authoritarian style would describe? Next, do the same read-through for the list of characteristics for children in these types of families. This will give you a better view of where you are as a parent. You could have your child read the parenting descriptions, but this author cautions against that as teenagers will almost always slide their perceptions toward the authoritarian style as they are seeking autonomy and can have a "pendulum effect" when assessing their own parents.

If you really want to know another perception of your style and you have a good, relaxed relationship with one of your child's friends...ask them. You may hear "You are strict, but not nearly as strict as my parents." But notice the shift. Every teenager thinks their parents are more strict than those of their friends...especially when they are asking for an exception to a family rule! The value in this activity lies in assessing the traits for who you *really* are and not who you wish to be. General descriptions of each type are listed below:

Authoritarian Parents

- Preservation of hierarchy and structure is paramount
- Emotional responses to the child's needs come second to the order of the house
- Parent strictly enforces rules and procedures in family with no negotiations
- Parent exercises change in rules according to their own logic and does not share reasoning with child when asked
- There individual boundaries and opinions of children are secondary to parents
- Privileges (phone, games, visits with friends) are taken away for punishment of infractions that may not have a direct link to the response
- Extrinsic motivation is acknowledged or utilized
- Excessive supervision of child's social functions
- Question the knowledge or experience of the teacher, assignment requirements, due dates, etc.

Permissive (Indulgent or Indifferent) Parents

- Do not maintain rules or procedures of family function
- Have few or no responsibilities or limits (chores, curfews, routines) for the child

- Highly responsive to child's emotional needs...to the point of compromising family procedures and expectations
- Act on assumption that only external natural consequences in the environment are needed for discipline
- Adjust rules of family to avoid emotional response or tantrums from the child
- Provide few boundaries with all opinions (parents and children) being equal
- Little or no supervision with the child's social functions
- Take on the role of "friend" with the child and his peers in social settings
- May do homework **for** the child rather than receive natural consequence
- Do not follow through on supporting teacher in the classroom nor on goals set during conferences

Authoritative Parents

- Have consistent and clearly defined expectations with some negotiation
- Child is involved in discipline, but parents retain decisions
- Emotionally responsive to child while maintaining expectations as separate from affection
- Parent shares reasoning used to make decisions, but decisions not negotiable
- If discipline involves removal of privileges, the consequence is aligned with the infraction (i.e. video game time removed because child was playing them instead of doing homework)
- Discussion is encouraged, but respect for roles and experience are upheld
- All family members have individual opinions that are acknowledged and supported; but not equally applied in decisions for the family
- Intrinsic motivation is encouraged and utilized
- Express moderated supervision when necessary

And what characteristics typically develop in the children raised with these parenting styles? The following are the patterns of qualities found in research over the years:

Children of Authoritarian Parents

- As students, they are extrinsically motivated
- Display lack of self-confidence in problem-solving and tasks
- Low levels of efficacy and autonomy
- Tend to be anxious and withdrawn in social and class settings
- Express high levels of frustration with difficult tasks
- Grades earned in school are directly reflective of parent involvement
- Have great difficulty with changes in environment

Children of Permissive (Indulgent or Indifferent) Parents

- Display lack of impulse control
- Have difficulty understanding boundaries, procedures, classroom rules
- Have low social competence
- Give up quickly with difficult tasks
- High frustration levels when encountering challenges in academics
- Tend to earn lower grades than children raised with authoritative style
- Do not respond appropriately (task-irrelevant) to changes in environment

Children of Authoritative Parents

- Have a well-developed sense of efficacy
- Advocate well for self, including seeing teachers when help is needed
- Social skills are highly developed
- Tend to earn higher grades than children raised with other two styles
- Good at regulating emotions according to situation
- Highly adaptive to changes in environment
- Have higher rates of persistence with difficult tasks

Studies consistently find that authoritative parenting styles (versus authoritarian or permissive) tend to generate the most successful outcomes in child performance in the classroom. These parents use approaches and techniques that foster development of problem-solving skills, and participation in decisions where choices are available. They also structure the family dynamics with clear and consistent expectations for behaviors and achievement (Grolnick, 1989). There is a fine line between involvement and intrusiveness. And, this line moves as the child develops into an adult. When our children are young, they want and require a high level of involvement from parents. As they approach the pre-teen years, a shift begins to occur in which the child is building her own autonomy and efficacy. In order to "step in" and effectively manage their own lives, this means that parents are required to " take a step back". A slow progression of disengagement from decisions needs to occur. **ALL** parents have difficulty with this process. If they didn't, it would mean that they weren't involved and dedicated to their younger child in the first place. But now the child is a teenager. The situation has changed. And the parent must change along with the environment and the child if the healthy, competent adult is to emerge.

Your parenting style as you perceive it: _____

Your parenting style as your teen perceives it: _____

The parenting style you observed in your parents: _____

Traits you like in your parenting style: _____

Traits you'd rather change in your style: _____

Reflections on Parenting Styles

Which patterns in your parenting style are similar to how your parents functioned?

_____

_____

_____

Which patterns in your parenting style are different from how your parents functioned?

_____

_____

_____

Are there characteristics in your style that elicit responses in your child that are not aligned with the goals you have set in raising him/her?

_____

If so, what are some techniques you could alter and begin to apply that might generate a more positive response in your teenager?

_____

_____

_____

TWO WEEK CHALLENGE:

After applying the changes in the question above, what results have you observed in the response of your teenager?

_____

_____

~ Day 5 ~

CALIBRATING THE COMPASS

Teenagers love food. More than anything. It's like a magnet, which means we can use it to attract them to the activity for this day (and hopefully all the days that follow). Food is a wonderful conversation center piece, because they are so enthralled with consuming treats that they scarcely notice anything else in the room. Set up a once a week (or every other week) "coffee/ice cream/frozen yogurt time" with your child. This is a time when just you and your child (siblings occupied elsewhere) have a reserved moment of disengagement from friends, activities, stresses, deadlines, games, etc. Even a 30 minute break would be constructive, but an hour is recommended. Don't be surprised if the first few times with these conversations seem forced and scripted. This is typical, because they are. But once they become common, they will evolve a genuine tone of interaction between the two of you. Once the designated time becomes routine, you may be amazed at the things your child is willing to disclose. Many psychologists identify the two most favorable times for teenagers to express their thoughts as being right before going to sleep and whenever you are driving in the car with your child. Both are times when teenagers feel emotionally safe, and yet not stuck in an intense face-to-face interaction (Riera, 2003).

This is typically a great time for them to ask you questions as well. Don't forget the old psychology vantage point…even when someone is asking you a question…they are also **telling** you something! Also during these designated quality times, it is very hard for most parents to remove themselves from the "lecture" mode. This is a time to listen. **Listen, listen, listen**! And listening is not black and white…it has shades of gray. For example, if your child says, "One of my friends tried some pot the other day." And you quickly respond with a defensive, "Well that was a dumb decision. Where did this occur? Did **YOU** try it?" Now the discussion has turned into an inquisition…and your child will likely respond by clamming up! In order to keep the lines of honest communication open, allow your child to express how he feels about using pot…and how he feels about the friend…and everything in between. This is what you were hoping for...openness and honesty. It comes with a price...knowledge that is sometimes more than we wanted to know.

Your reaction will determine whether these meeting times will become buoys for communication and strengthening your child's skills...or times that force a chasm between the two of you. And this doesn't mean acquiescing into agreement or even neutrality about the subject. There will be time outside the safe boundary of the designated quality time to get your point across. Besides, your child already *knows* your position on the matter. What they may really be saying is, "I'm not sure how to navigate this friendship anymore because my buddy is doing something I don't want to do." Or even, "I'm concerned about my buddy....do you think this habit will negatively impact him in the long run?" Now there is truly value in this level of communication. Rather than lecture, ask questions. "Are you concerned about your buddy?" "Did it make you feel uneasy being there?" Try to turn your statements into questions ...that is, if you want answers.

~ Day 6 ~

THE SONG OF THE SIRENS

The song of the sirens was deadly for Homer in *The Odyssey*. You may feel the same about your teenager's music. But nonetheless, knowing the message behind the music may help guide us through some treacherous waters. Ask your child who his/her **three** favorite musical artists are. Then, go to either Amazon.com or iTunes and *listen* to the top selling songs of those artists. The top-selling songs are designated at these sites. And even if the lyrics make your ears bleed...*listen*! For whatever reason, those songs are "speaking" to your child...something key is identified in those lyrics or that melody. This guidebook encourages you to ask further questions about the meanings behind those lyrics as well...but avoid expressing judgment to your child! As hard as it may be, keep from judging their selection of music and lyrics. Otherwise, it may be the last time your child tells you anything about their musical preferences! Second, ask your child to tell you three musical groups or artists that some of their peers listen to...but he/she cannot stand. Then, ask WHY these artists are on the "out" list for your child. Granted, you may get an answer that is as innocuous as "I just don't like their sound." Or, "Their lyrics are repetitive and boring." OK. But what does that mean to your child?

In learning what is mundane to your child, you may find yourself pleasantly relieved to find that they actually know musical quality when they hear it. But perhaps, the answers you receive are very powerful...loaded with information about their daily habits, ethics, levels of violence, political views, etc. Wouldn't it be a breath of fresh air to know that like you, your child also sees a certain group as having lyrics that are negative about women? Or that your child *used to* listen to an artist, but then read an internet article about how the lead musician used weapons against the spouse in their home...and, as a result, now your child doesn't listen to that group anymore. Very revealing, right? In the early 90's, I was observing select groups of students who frequently wore black t-shirts with album logos from the band, Nirvana. I had seen pictures of the members with their thick eyeliner and dingy plaid shirts...and initially blew them off as an angry iconoclastic band. Then one student prompted me to read some of their lyrics...and I was impressed with the depth of reflection and layers of meaning in Kurt Cobain's poetry...yes, poetry. I never saw that band the same way again...nor the students who listened to their music or wore their t-shirts. Those students were "my deep thinkers"...they held a lot of idealism about social structure, and were intense in their emotional connections with life experiences...but they weren't angry...and they weren't reactionary. They were amazing.

~ Day 7 ~

NAUTICAL FLAGS AND THEIR MEANINGS

Whether they are bumper stickers on the car, in the locker, on their bedroom door, hanging from the backpack zipper, or on their laptops and notebooks...they aren't there for aesthetic decoration. Teenagers are far too myopic into their own worlds to care what others outside their circle think of them...such masters at conservation of effort! The symbols are methods of communication...but with teens, they are **primary** methods of communication ...to their peers and to society.

Not so long ago, drawing the symbol for "anarchy" on notebooks was a big thing with some teenagers. As teachers, we thought this was pretty funny, as most of our students couldn't *really* define anarchy accurately. What they were actually describing about the symbol was iconoclastic or anti-establishmentarian action. They wanted to challenge the system. Just like all teenagers in all generations. We weren't concerned anymore that they were planning some kind of coup. Become familiar with the meanings of their symbols. Then, make note of which celebrities are also brandishing these same symbols on their clothing, with tattoos, on music covers, etc.

As teenagers increase their circle of individuals and their vocabulary increases so that they can more accurately express themselves in other venues, they tend to move away from the symbols. Note that most college students are usually phasing-out the "symbols" as a primary means of signaling peers and identifying people of similar views. For them, symbols have been replaced with something absolutely amazing...literacy.

In the space below, draw three to five symbols found on your teen's personal belongings:

Next, use "Google Images" to find the associations and meanings of these symbols. Which celebrities associate with these as well? Which websites contain these? Do other peers in your child's class display these same symbols on their backpacks, car bumpers, laptops, or notebooks? And, what are these peers like in terms of social interactions and academic achievement? Now you are really learning the information conveyed in which flags we fly!

~ Day 8 ~

HOW TO AVOID WALKING THE PLANK

Psychologist David Walsh actually uses a one-line metaphor of sailing to describe an incredibly easy and successful way of avoiding power struggles with a teenager. "When you feel like taking the wind out of his sails, it is a better idea to take YOUR sails out of his wind", meaning several things, actually (Walsh, 2004). First, you are the one who does not have a limbic system on impulsive overload. You are the one with a fully-matured pre-frontal cortex. This means that avoiding a power struggle, or the escalation of one, is entirely up to you...not your teen. Second, let him vent. Because adolescents are so emotionally driven, they have a greater want (I didn't say 'need') to be heard than you do. You have a need to be heard so that your teen can mature successfully with your guidance. But from his/her perspective, the teenager's "wants" come first. This doesn't mean allowing the tantrum to take over...just to let it blow out. Let the energy (and the adrenaline) depreciate in effect so that he will be ready to actually listen to your "words of wisdom".

Below is a list of guiding principles to manage a productive conversation with teenagers. Because we can't predict when a conflict will arise (nor would be *want* to), the activity for today will actually need to occur when the situation calls for it. But, to help you reflect later on whether you were able to employ a few of these, use the indicated space at the end of this section to make a small note on the topic of the conflict, and how you observed the application of these skills. This will be a bit like reviewing notes on Monday Night Football. (Where's the beer commercial when you need it?)

Allow your teenager to talk first...remember the requirements of the limbic system? A teenager will not...and cannot...listen to anyone until the emotional needs of being heard have been met. Any talking before this on your part is just wasted effort. Or worse, the teen could shut down completely and dismiss the entire discussion. Another way to look at this technique is from the perspective of how the issue started in the first place. Most likely, it was due to a lack of problem-solving skills in doing a chore or upholding a family rule; or it could have been generated by an emotional response. So, making sure that what you have to say does not become something that the teenager can accidently turn to further amplify their already-heightened emotional state would actually avoid complicating an already convoluted mess.

Whenever possible, allow the child to be part of the solution. This helps them build their problem-solving skills, which are lagging behind thanks to the developmental rate of that pre-frontal cortex we discussed earlier. Adolescence also need to feel a sense of self-efficacy, that their voices are heard. From their perspective, we keep asking them to act like adults and make decisions. Once they do so, we either question their judgment or ignore it (and invalidate it) altogether. No wonder so many teenagers say "I just can't win with you!" Another benefit to including the teen in the solution is the personal accountability that goes along with the actions and any outcomes from the solution. If they are part of the game, they will stay in the game.

If your teen has displayed a behavior or action that is not what you hoped for, rather than using a judgmental or punitive tone, try using "I statements". For example, rather than saying, "You are home late again!" Another possibility is, "I get worried about you when you arrive later than you agreed to in our earlier conversation. I don't want to worry; and I want to know I can rely on your words." Now you have removed the "finger-pointing" and actually gone to the two main points of concern: safety and trust.

As with adults (and any human being at any stage of life), it is important to convey unconditional love and support whether a resolution is reached regarding the conflict or not. There is nothing productive about leaving a concern with added emotional concerns. Remember that risk-taking and exploration of new territories is all part of expanding the mind into the adult world. If they didn't extend beyond their current boundaries, they would never grow. But in venturing beyond familiar territory, they are actually quite frightened. And, the worst thing, in their minds, that they could do to sabotage their autonomy would be to come home asking for your reassurance. The irony is, of course, that they need it now more than ever.

And finally, give the teenager "room for retreat". Remember that all animals need a place to feel safe, a place they can predictively control, a place that can **temporarily** remove them from stresses (or confrontations) to allow for time to process or cool-down. Keep poking an opossum and the result is not hard to imagine. (I specifically used the opossum because, as a teacher, there are many times that angry teens have seemed very similar to angry opossums from my viewpoint.) There's nothing wrong with either party indicating a need for a few minutes (or hours) to gain a productive perspective on a situation. What is important, however, is that a communication is made regarding **when** the problem-solving discussion can resume so that no one feels that they are left hanging without validation. Then no one is left "hanging" with unresolved issues. In fact, skilled teachers will use this technique knowing that there will be **FOUR** beneficial outcomes: If a student has an "off-task behavior" during class, sometimes the best method of handling the situation is to calmly say to the student, "Johnny, I'd like to see you after class." This does not in any way communicate a lack of classroom management on the teacher's part....actually, just the opposite. The teacher is conveying to the student, "Your behavior **will** be addressed, but it is **not** important enough to derail the learning in this classroom. I will continue teaching, and the focus will not be on your behavior." Second, the child is given time...time to reflect on the behavior, whether or not it was worth it, and what-on-Earth the teacher may or may not say or do at the end of class. This void of "not-knowing" is absolute torture to a teenager. And guess who has re-established the authority in the room? That same void of not knowing will also work on the rest of the students in the room observing the behavior...and taking note of the teacher's calm, calculated response. The third and fourth benefits are actually for the teacher. This course of action gives the teacher time to disengage his or her limbic system from the response that will occur later. It also gives the teacher plenty of time to think about the most logical and productive response available...time to carefully and confidently weigh options. For parents, this could be as simple as saying, "We will discuss this first thing in the morning." My own father cost me lots of sleep many times with that one! And, his point was never lost throughout the night...it was accentuated.

CONFLICT RESOLUTION REFLECTION

1. What was the conflict regarding? _____

2. What was the initial emotional state of your teen?
    _____
    _____
    _____

3. Were you able to allow your teenager to "vent" first? _____
    Why or why not? _____

4. Which techniques did you select to use for this conflict? _____
    _____
    _____
    _____

5. Which techniques worked well? _____
    _____
    _____

6. What was the final emotional state of your teen? _____
    _____
    _____

7. What was the resolution that was reached by both parties? _____
    _____
    _____

8. Do you feel that your teenager learned some valuable points about functioning more in the adult world as a result of this process? _____
    Why or why not? _____

~ Day 9 ~

"X" MARKS THE SPOT ON THE MAP

It's hard to find treasure if the landmarks on the path to the "X" are not clearly marked. Recall that the activity for day 9 was assessing the storm. Parents were asked, in part, to identify three behaviors exhibited by their teenager that could be improved to be more successful in achieving goals. These are the treasures we are trying to discover. For today, we can work on the landmarks to get there. In the earlier activity, the limitation of only three goals was important to reduce the feeling of being "picked-upon" and to narrow our focus on certain priorities.

When it comes to pre-teens and teenagers, they tend to have an obsession with fairness. Unfortunately, that fairness only applies to them and not in situations when their actions affect others (Riera, 2012). Behavioral contracts are one effective method for making very succinct definitions of the behavior desired. If there is a behavior to be avoided, it is more beneficial that the statement in the contract is changed to a desired one. For example, if you would like to influence your teenager to stop picking on her little sibling, one way to phrase this in a contract is with a goal statement such as the following: "Ashley will treat Teresa with respect by honoring the boundaries of her bedroom and speaking to her in a calm voice without the use of inappropriate words." Another example of a contract for a curfew time might be "I will respect my parents and the house rules by upholding the curfew time of 9:00 on weekends with a grace period of 15 minutes. If I call and speak to my parents at least 30 minutes before the curfew time lapses, it may be extended based on circumstances..."

There are several keys that can make behavioral contracts successful. The most important factor is consistency in not only upholding the disciplinary action if the contract is not fulfilled, but also in upholding any positive reinforcements that are fairly earned and delivered in a timely manner. Clearly stating expectations also keeps behaviors in an objective light, and not convoluted in emotions or judgments. Another key is to keep the goal behavior phrased with a positive tone and a brief description, but with enough detail that the teen does not feel that expectations are unclear. Time lines and days of expected completion are also necessary for clarity with both parties. For some teens, a small notecard with a brief contract on it is all that is necessary...nothing formal.

For today's activity, select the three behaviors and, together with your teenager, draft behavior contracts that will help clarify what the expectations are and how the goals can be accomplished. Remember that consistency and objectivity are ingredients for success.

Examples of Behavior Contract Topics

- Each day I will have _____ total time with screen time (video games, TV, iPad, computer that is not homework related, etc.)...

- Once a week on _____ (day), I will clean my room before _____ (time), which will include _____ (specific chores to be completed)...

- I will participate in _____ (activity) as long as my grades are _____ (minimum) and my house duties are completed by _____ (day_...

- I will only use _____ minutes on my cell phone per month, or pay the difference by _____ (day) after the bill arrives. If I use the phone during school, the consequence will be _____. I will respond to parent calls or texts within _____ (time frame)...

- In order to have a hamster (cat, dog, rabbit, etc.), I have to take care of him. This means _____ (behaviors) daily and _____ (behaviors) weekly. If I do not care for him, a new home will be found that can give him the care he deserves to be happy and healthy.

- If my grade in _____ (specific class) drops below _____ (grade percent), then I will make arrangements to visit the teacher for help before or after school _____ (# times) in the week following the grade drop.

- In order to earn my allowance, I will complete the following chores of _____ by _____ each week before I attend social events with friends.

~ Day 10 ~

YOU CAN'T DIVE WITH FLOATIES ON

This next suggestion is actually about what **NOT** to do. As a child, did you ever try to retrieve something from the bottom of the pool with your floaties still hugging your upper arms? This presents a new challenge in which buoyancy is not your friend. It's time to dive...on your own. What once kept you out of trouble may actually hinder your progress. And, this is hard for us as parents to accept. If we don't modify our role in the lives of our teenagers, we can actually hinder their growth and success in developing skills to navigate in the bigger world. Ouch. But it's only an "ouch" if you interpret this shift in roles as centered on you and your old role of protector at a highly involved level. It's not about you...and a decrease in the level of involvement in parental care does not mean some other role doesn't take its place. It does. Now you are needed from the standpoint of a mentor. Don't go with the false conclusion that this means you aren't needed or wanted. You are. But not as a filter from the outside world. It's time for the teenager to experience this place that is waiting for him. And, it really is what you've been preparing for over the last 12-14 years!

The time has definitely come to take off the floaties. And keep this mantra in mind during tough moments when you are tempted to once again wrap tightly around your teenager's arm:

In _not_ doing something, we are providing the opportunity for our children do it.

Seriously...consider writing this sentence down on a notecard and taping it up somewhere on your mirror as a gentle reminder every morning. Also remember that "it" is the process of developing one's own autonomy and efficacy. If they do not feel they can swim and dive on their own...they can't. And if they develop a sense that they are powerless to control their own lives, they will become weak adults. This is also just like teaching them to walk. If you constantly hold their hand, they can't achieve balance nor build their leg muscles. And, the only way we learn to avoid a fall...is to fall. I know you've heard a million variations on this one, but it is absolutely true. This goes all the way back to (and even before) Erik Erikson's stages of psychosocial development (Erikson, 1968). Much of his initial work was adopted by and evolved into a refined view of the development of self in Howard Gardner's views on multiple intelligences, as well (Gardner, 2006). Why are these researchers important? Beyond their ideas, the application of their ideas in educational psychology and the classroom techniques used by so many teachers today is key to understanding what teachers are trying to accomplish "on the other side of the desk" where parents cannot venture. Students who experience authoritative parenting styles and who encounter teachers with authoritative classroom settings tend to build their own autonomy and to be self-regulated (Grolnick, 1989). If you are familiar with these researchers and their ideas, it can be reassuring to know that your child's teacher actually has the same goals for producing a competent, happy adult as the parents do. It's just hard for us as parents of teenagers to equate their adolescent experiences with learning to walk so long ago.

Try this additional visualization in moments when you are questioning whether you should take a step forward or take a step back: If you are teaching your child to drive, the easiest thing to do (when they are struggling) would be to simply have him jump in the passenger seat and have you take over. But now who is driving? Are his driving skills improving? Not at all. A perplexing observation I, and my colleagues, have been seeing in schools for the last decade or so involves the long-standing tradition of students decorating lockers for each other. They do this for birthdays, upcoming games, school events, etc. In my generation, we always gathered streamers, signs and balloons and hauled them to school in our backpacks. My peers and I would plan to meet at the designated locker of the lucky recipient just before school. This was an incredibly fun event, and built cohesiveness among our peer group, not to mention learning the valuable lesson of supporting each other in significant moments and just doing positive things for each other. Guess who frequently does the locker decorating now? Parents. An opportunity for growth is lost...and a fond memory of high school never happens.

We want our children to catch a breath in the turmoil of these choppy waves, right? Then that's what we need to let them do...breathe. If we are too close (you've heard of the "helicopter parent"), they can't find themselves because all they see...is you. Setting the routine quality time (from number 2) not only ensures a regular "checking-in"...but it also relieves your child from the worry or concern that parents are ALWAYS in his/her space. Because, now there are times that your teen can feel assured when you will **NOT** be "in his face". You may actually find that, with the scheduled time in place, you don't feel like "hovering" quite so much. This is good for both parent and teen! But be prepared...it doesn't feel comfortable because this is a new role for you as a parent.

So for today's activity, consciously choose three situations in which you actually step back and let your teen step up. Maybe the task will involve doing their own laundry, or washing the dishes, or advocating for herself with a teacher or boss (without your intervention), or setting-up their own checking account. But the challenge for today would be meaningless if we simply do it this one day, and then revert back to taking control of the car...or putting the floaties back on. The real challenge is in making a permanent change from this point forward! So, think very carefully about the three major areas in which you feel it is time to take a step back. It is even a good idea to discuss these with your teenager and decide the three actions together. As you ponder which ones to select, try to think of the skills your child needs as s/he enters the adult world. Then list them on the following page as a reminder to you that these are now part of your new role as the parent of a teenager!

Removing the Floaties Activity

Example #1:

Floatie Removed: I will no longer change the bed sheets for my child.

New Skill for My Teen: He will now take charge and remove, wash, and replace his own sheets once a week, as he can now care for his own bedding. Once this is accomplished by Friday, he can enjoy socializing for the weekend.

Example #2:

Floatie Removed: I will no longer shop for my teen's clothes at the beginning of the school year.

New Skill for My Teen: He will now take charge of selecting his own clothing when I give him a gift card at the beginning of the school year with a limited amount, and he has to decide **how** to spend the money wisely on clothing(and learn the value of some of the clothes he is selecting). He will then show me his purchases, which still need parental approval for appropriateness at school.

Floatie #1 Removed: _____

New Skill for My Teen: _____

_____

Floatie #2 Removed: _____

New Skill for My Teen: _____

_____

Floatie #3 Removed: _____

New Skill for My Teen: _____

_____

There is something else to consider in your choices. Take another look at example #2. This author employed this same technique when my teenage son and I had encountered one too many arguments over how "my selection of his shirts was not cool". I was upset because I was spending good money on shirts that were not being worn, but hung in the closet with the tags still on them! In taking a step back, I realized that as long as I had the final say on whether the clothes were appropriate or not, he could...and should...be making these decisions on his own. And, I was limiting the amount spent to what I would normally supply at the beginning of a school year anyway. Amazingly, this not only worked well and freed me from the burden of shopping for him (which was the unexpected bonus), but the arguments about item selections and clothing usage came to a wonderfully abrupt end! Once we were no longer arguing constantly about clothing details, the flow of conversations in our weekly coffee dates (day 4 activity) became more pleasant as well!

Reflections on the effects and benefits you have observed in both your teenager and you after "removing the floaties":

_____

_____

_____

_____

_____

_____

Relationships:

Peers

As with any vessel, a seasoned and knowledgeable crew can actually run the ship even if a captain is temporarily detained or distracted. They know the expectations of the captain, are mindful of the charted course, and are completely familiar with all the equipment on board. As long as there are no immediate changes or drastic maneuvers required, they are very competent and adept at sailing along. A "bad" crew, on the other hand, might be recently acquired sailors who really don't know the routines aboard, are unaware of the course (or don't have the same course as the captain), and could easily mutiny the destination or worse...sink the ship.

Each of us is the captain of our own ship. Our peers, friends, serve as crew that know the course we have charted. Good friends support your efforts and encourage the positive direction you travel. They are familiar with your strengths and weaknesses, and can work with them to produce the best outcome for your journey. And, really good friends can even keep us on course when we have moments of uncertainty, encounter becalmed waters (apathy, depression, loss of volition or motivation), or even get flat-out lost. Sometimes they are even the first to alert us that we are no longer on course! Teenagers do not yet fully understand the value of solid, positive friendships. For one thing, teenagers don't even know **themselves** well yet...which means they are changing course all the time. How can a person select good friends if they don't know their own qualities, strengths and limitations yet? And, teens do not have enough **experience** in their lives to select friends wisely. The criteria they use for selection can be astounding at times. Ever notice how elementary aged children select friends based on favorite colors, favorite movies...things they are experiencing in the world around them?

Teenagers tend to select the friends with similar angst and issues. As they progress through high school, these shift more toward college and career interests. It's not a coincidence that they now select their courses based primarily on the best preparatory tract for their adult lives as opposed to the teacher they think is "cool" or the "nicest", as middle school children do. Another factor of selection is that their *friends* have not had enough experiences for others to assess their true character, either. You're not sure what you're getting...because what you are getting in that friend...changes frequently. In fact, teachers are not at all surprised to hear that friendship circles have altered radically at every entry level of school...the first year of middle school, after which comes the first year of high school, the first year of college...then again right after college graduation, when careers and financial demands are coming into view.

At each of these stages, new variables have been introduced into their lives. It's time to reassess goals...and redraft the charted course...maybe even get a new crew. This is a good time for parents to be very observant of the new crew, because it will be based on the new direction of travel. Sometimes it is a very positive new direction that indicates more stability and maturity. Other times, it is an alert that there are storms ahead. Either way, it's good to remember that teens spend less and less time in port now...and more time sailing with the crew. Guess which has more day-to-day influence?

Another type of equipment that influences your course when sailing would include any navigational instruments. In today's society, this would be social media, cell phones, texting, Facebook, Instagrams, etc. A 2009 study by Dr. Scott Frank found that hyper-texting teens, defined as those who write more than 120 texts per day, are 25% more likely to report high levels of stress and 40% more likely to indicate symptoms of depression (McLeod, 2011). There is a positive correlation between the number of texts sent by teens and those who are more unhappy, bored, or get into trouble (Rideout, 2010). In addition to emotional concerns with the disconnect of direct communication for electronic messaging, we also have to consider the factor of cyberbullying. Over 75% of all teenagers in the U.S. have a cell phone. Almost 25% of teenagers report being *routinely* threatened by a peer through social media. Over half of all teens with social media have been witness to it in a peripheral position. And specifically, a study conducted in 2010 reported 54% of LGBT youths were victims of cyberbullying within the last 30 days (Blumenfeld, 2010). One of the activities in this section will be about temporarily disengaging from the cell phone at certain times. Many adolescents today have these devices with them 24-7, and literally do not know how to function easily without them. If any form of cyberbullying is occurring, one of the first courses of action would be to remove the offending instrument. This would at least give a person time to get centered, reflect on a course of action, and allow rational problem-solving to put into perspective what has been exacerbated by emotional responses going back and forth between parties.

And, until we get into more detail about cell phones in a later chapter, consider documenting below the number of texts your teenager sends in one day...one week...one month. How does this volume compare to yours?

~ Day 11 ~

HOLD FIRM THE WHEEL AND THE RUDDER

Since the pre-frontal cortex is still under construction in teenagers, we are sometimes amazed at their path of logic in finding solutions to problems, especially social ones involving peers. These types of issues have magnified risks and implications for friendships, social functions, being a member of a school team, etc. Sometimes as parents, one thing we really want to know is, "What will my child actually do if a situation arises?" Will s/he hold firm to the wheel, meaning will he maintain his/her course and not allow peer pressure to affect his/her better judgment? Will his/her decision and course of action show signs of principles you have addressed at home, or will those be thrown overboard? In the activity for day 11, you will be asked to give your child five "scenarios" that are you have already established as "undesirable". For each scenario, ask your child what he/she thinks the best decision or response would be if your child were actually in the dilemma. Then listen to the level of reflective thought and preventative action (or lack thereof) that do into each answer as you listen.

Scenario one is a party at a friend's house where alcohol is being served. While it is tempting, avoid asking your child whether they would accept the alcohol...the most likely answer is, of course, "no" when asked by a parent, regardless of the actions that truly would be taken at the time of the event. Instead, ask your child **how** he/she might avoid actually drinking the alcohol, and what your child would say to a friend trying to encourage taking a drink. If the answer is immediate, without depth, and lacking plausibility in today's social structure, that is reason for some concern. If, on the other hand, your child says something reflective, clever, and reveals the true nature of peer interactions...that's better. And best of all, if your child actually says, "This is what I say or do in those situations...". While you may not take comfort in the fact that these moments have already been presented to your child, keep in mind that these are inevitable. And your child has just revealed not only their "technique" for handling matters, but the fact that they actually DO handle them!   Remember that there are no "absolutely correct" answers to these questions.

As parents, we know what we prefer as an outcome in most of these, but the true knowledge is in listening to **how** your teenager's reasoning is flowing through the course of these problem-solving activities. This is a prime opportunity to observe how they think. The less you say and the more they describe, the more meaningful the knowledge you will receive. And, many of these are situations in which it could seem that there is no easy way out. Life is full of these moments. We want to see what the performance and response might be. And, as with many of the activities in this guidebook, since this is linked to the development of the pre-frontal cortex, consider revisiting these questions in six months or in the next school year to see how your adolescent has progressed in social awareness, problem-solving, and critical thinking skills.

As you prepare for the activities that follow, consider asking your teenager "binary questions" in which they are given two choices (either both negative; or both positive) and have to select one over the other. This will give you a peek into their prioritization skills. Remember these are all hypotheticals with no correct answer, only opinions.

Example: Would you rather lose your cell phone for a week or your car for a day?

Example: Would you rather go to a small college and play on the field often, or go to a large college and not have as many opportunities to play on the field?

PROBLEM-SOLVING SITUATIONS

1. You are at a party at a friend's house where alcohol is being served. How will you avoid drinking if your peers decide to do so? What will you say to your friends the next day? What are the chances that the next party could have not just alcohol, but other drugs?

2. Your friend shows you a text in which she is bullied. This is the tenth time it has happened today. What do you do? Do you tell any adults? Why or why not? Do you speak to the person who has been sending the messages? Why or why not?

3. One of your friends cheated on a major class project, and you are aware of it. What do you do? Do you report it? Why or why not? If you decide to report it, to whom do you tell? How would you go about reporting it? Do you speak directly with your friend about the incident?

4. You are feeling pressure from your boyfriend/girlfriend to participate in more involved sexual activity than you are personally comfortable with at this time (this could be any type...intercourse, oral sex, etc. so the type is purposefully vague in the phrasing of the question). But he/she continues to pressure you when you go out on dates. What do you say to this person? What do you think of the person you are dating? Will you tell any adult about the situation? Why or why not?

5. Which of the following situations do you consider to be "worse"...and **WHY**?

   - Drinking alcohol or smoking pot
   - Having oral sex or having intercourse
   - Lying to your best friend or lying to a parent
   - Stealing money or stealing possessions?
   - Hurting your friend's feelings or having your feelings hurt?
   - Having parents who care too much or who don't care at all?
   - Taking a "fun" class that is "challenging" or taking a "boring" class that is "easy"?
   - Cramming for a test and losing sleep or not cramming and getting enough sleep (in both situations you don't feel adequately prepared for the test)?

~ Day 12 ~
A STEADY CREW

The truth about the successful voyage of any ship is, in large part, due to the competence and dedication of the crew. Even if the captain is very knowledgeable and skilled, those abilities cannot extend to running all of the stations required to keep the ship moving on course. For our teenagers, we know how influential their friends can be in their thoughts and actions. Unfortunately, changing friendship circles goes with the territory of trying out different roles as teenagers transition from childhood to adulthood. Thus, they will be making critical selections of very important people at a time when they are most unsure of themselves and most vulnerable to outside influences. No wonder we, as parents, get nervous about the saying "Birds of a feather flock together" if some of our child's friends seem off-track in one way or another.

In day 12, you are encouraged to ask about your child's best friend(s). But be specific. Simply asking, "Why do you like Ben?" may get you a circular logic answer coupled with a look of "Duh." "Because he's my friend." Or you may get the obvious, "Because he's nice." Again, "Duh." Consider the following, "What are three **traits** that make this person a good friend to you?" Not only will this subtle change in phrasing concentrate the attention on personality qualities your child admires and gravitates toward, but also focuses your *child* on considering the qualities in people rather than just outcomes or superficial exchanges in society.

Many times, both as parents and as teachers, we forget the power in simply asking a question. Simply posing a question alters the direction and involvement of a conversation...and the path of thoughts in the person being addressed. Here's a quick example in the classroom: If a student is frustrated with a situation to the edge of tears (let's say the student is hurt by what is perceived as social exclusion by a friend) , not only do we want to avoid that level of emotional pain and stress to crescendo in the classroom (or anywhere), but as teachers, we also realize that a student could feel embarrassed very quickly if their emotions take over their actions. In an effort to help the student regain a cognitive focus and avoid embarrassment, I will first dignify her feelings by saying, "That would definitely hurt anyone. I can understand your feelings." But I will quickly add a question that refocuses the student away from the emotional situation and directs her to think about positive aspects of her own character. "Have you ever had that moment when you did something, and it had an effect on someone else that you didn't intend?" Now the student has been given the opportunity to think from a different perspective. Another example is, "I've seen what a good friend you are to others in class. What do **you** do to make a friend feel better when they are sad?" In this response, the student has been alerted to one of her own strengths...and redirected to think of past situations in which she was the one providing strength and guidance. At this point, it becomes much easier for her to assume the lead in her own situation as well.

Trait One in Friends: _____

Why is this valued? _____

_____

Trait Two in Friends: _____

Why is this valued? _____

_____

Trait Three in Friends: _____

Why is this valued? _____

_____

~ Day 13 ~

THE LINE IN THE SAND

Now for the inverse of what we encountered for day 12, which will actually tell us twice as much as the previous activity. Ask your child to describe five traits that would be "friendship breakers". If there have been past experiences when this actually occurred, use those as a starting point. "You used to be friends with Johnny in middle school...what happened?" The tempting part here is to ask about why these are breakers...but be careful not to pry into the zone of judging your child's peer group.

Remember that the strongest point of immediate influence on a teenager's decisions and behaviors is their peer group. In telling you about traits that are determining factors of members of that circle, your child is revealing the layers of their psyche and emotional security boundaries. "This I cannot tolerate...even if I have cared about you in the past." And that's a big, big deal.

Friendship Breaker One: _____

Friendship Breaker Two: _____

Friendship Breaker Three: _____

~ Day 14 ~

CROSSING THE PRIME MERIDIAN

Sailors use mapping coordinates that are based on several reference points: the equator, the stars, and the prime meridian. The last one is the 0° longitude point (running through Greenwich, England) from which time zones are also calculated. The activity for this day is called "time zones" because it related to how we spend our time and the quality of those minutes.

In today's society, it's hard to discern quality time from a lack thereof, as many things are not in "real time". We record shows we can't watch at the time of broadcast. Even when we send text messages, there is sometimes a delay between sending and receiving times. And technology, while it allows us to conduct communication at a faster rate than ever before, is also an obstacle that intrudes on our most precious of elements that we cannot regain once passed...time. As parents, we didn't know about anything _**but**_ real time growing up. The only thing that could even come close to altering time was the instant replay on Monday night football...that was a new technology! Now we are at the twenty yard line!" Wow. We ARE old, relatively. Social media, including texting, Facebook, and Instagram (to name just a few), all impose on our actual, live time communicating face-to-face. And, in the wake of these technological advancements, it is not unusual to observe people out at a local pastry shop or having dinner at a restaurant...and using their various modes of technology rather than talking to the person who is actually present at the table! To give you a sense of perspective, teenagers in the U.S. generate over 3,300 texts per month (Fisch, 2013).

The activity for today is to set aside just 30 minutes of time when both you and your teenager are "off the grid" and disconnected from any electronic devices. Another study found that teenagers spend an average of 8.5 hours per day using digital devices and social media, which was an increase of greater than 30% from just three years prior to the study.

Additionally, 30% of the time they are actually using more than one devise simultaneously (Rideout, 2010). The plasticity of the brain begins to rapidly diminish in our early to mid-20s. The concern now is the potential effect of losing this window of opportunity to develop all the other skills the human brain needs when such an inordinate amount of time is now devoted to technology alone.

The suggested setting for this activity is one that also does not distract you from each other. For example, a walk around the lake, a dessert picnic at the park, or visiting an outdoor monument...but not attending an activity. Those tend to grab a person's focus. All you have is each other....and communication. Below, consider a brief reflection of what you and your teen actually discussed and accomplished during this moment in "real-time". If it was peaceful and productive, who knows? Maybe it will become a ritual for you with other family members as well!

Reflection on Time Zones Activity:

_____

_____

_____

_____

_____

_____

_____

_____

~ Day 15 ~

THE LOOKOUT ON THE POOP DECK

This activity will receive the response of "You want me to chaperone what?!?" from most parents. The term "poop deck" actually comes from the Latin word puppis, meaning "stern". The poop deck is simply located at the stern (front) of the ship. No actual reference to bodily functions exists here, even though many teenagers would find that humorous. Of course, the sailor on the poop deck is looking for anything the captain needs to see from a distance...land, icebergs, other ships. This sailor is well trained and experienced at identifying trouble before it begins. Guess who that has to be in your teen's life. Yep...up to the poop deck you go! No one can do this job better than you. Why? Well, it's not so much for the obstacles in the water that we are using this analogy for today's activity, it's because the person on the poop deck is above the main deck and can also see...the other sailors. Are they doing their jobs? Are they a positive influence on the captain, or are they inadvertently steering the ship in the wrong direction? Do they have another agenda, or are their actions aligned with steering the ship where it needs to go? From the vantage point high atop the main mast, these things can readily be seen. This is the perfect position for a parent wanting to assess how their teenager's friends are influencing the direction in which your child is traveling.

Schools and school events always need chaperones to not only assist with the mechanics of the events, but to keep an eye of safety on the teenagers. Sponsors will always call on parents to assist in these activities, as faculty members are almost always in short supply. This is not a plea to fulfill a civic duty...this is a moment of opportunity for you. No, it's not about eavesdropping on your teenager, either. In fact, a healthy distance between you and your child at the event will allow each of you some space to explore and not impede the natural flow of things. So then why chaperone the assembly, prom, the soccer banquet, the freshman cookout? There are two main reasons other than simply being able to see those with whom your child associates.

First, this is a terrific opportunity for you to meet other parents and further develop your support group of other parents suffering similar fates in the storms of adolescence. It's a guarantee that you will come away from these conversations with assurance that you are not alone. This, alone, is wonderful therapy! You may even get a few solid leads from parents who have already raised a child or two through the obstacle course. But the second reason is that you are placed in the perfect "observation tower" for comparisons of adolescent behavior. Now you get to see how the "typical" teenager acts...when around other teenagers! Just think about the first Harlow monkey studies when scientists were watching individuals isolated in cages without any physical connection or attachment. Then compare the quality and context of those observations with the interactions that could be observed once all of the members of the troop were together. Now you're talking Dian Fossey and Jane Goodall. Put together the scientists who previously studied individual effects in the 50's and 60's with those monitoring social effects in the 70's and 80's...and you now have Robert Sapolsky, who is currently connecting the dots between multiple levels of effect. Brilliant. So, the challenge for day 10 is to find the school or district or team calendar, and select an event that is calling for chaperones...and mark the date! You will get to walk in the shoes of Sapolsky; although he gives his baboons a sedation dart using a blow gun. I do not advise this method with teenagers...even at the prom dance.

PRE-EVENT:
Event I am courageously chaperoning: _____

POST-EVENT:
What are the observations I noticed from a distance? _____

_____

_____

Relationships:
Teachers

Let's return to a scenario presented in the PREFACE of this guidebook. A parent is contacting the teacher, concerned that her son has dyed his hair blue. Blue is a color, not a core change in personality. It could indicate a number of things...most of them fairly benign and even entertaining in our society. The teacher inherently knows to look for OTHER behaviors that have been correlated...or not correlated...with things that can or should distress us. Frequently, the teacher also has a very good idea of which other teenagers are in the circle of peer influence for your child...NOT the ones we are TOLD are their friends...but the ones who actually ARE influencing them on a daily basis. And THIS is very critical information.

And the astute teacher will extend those observations beyond the classroom based on the extra-curricular activities and conversations held by the teenagers about which musical artists they listen to...and admire, which places they frequent for socializing and parties, and many other factors indicating the direction of the thought processes going on behind those confused, intense adolescent eyes.

Teachers are good at identifying the current music and artists admired by their students. I'm sorry, but I do not personally appreciate the music of a specific pop icon that our teenagers are currently following...nor her twerking. I'm more of a James Taylor and Jackson Browne kind of person. But as a teacher, I needed to know what all of my students were chattering about on Youtube. During passing periods between classes, they are all glued to their cell phones and twittering details and responses to "the incident."

There are also many methods used by teenagers to convey many, many things...musical preference, social groups, sexual behavior, drug activity, and so on. And, the reality of the teenager's world is a very myopic and immediate one. They forget that their teachers are in the halls...observing locker doors, notebook covers, keychain objects, shirt logos, etc. I remember changing my shirt (from the nice polo to the black rock-n-roll logo) in the car on the way to school (yes, while driving...safe, huh?!?) and adding the second set of earrings to my double-pierced ears that eluded my mother and father. The child who pulled out of the driveway was not the exact same child who walked into her first hour class. And my teacher knew it.

It's a different world today. And, according to Karl Fisch, Scott McLeod and the group XPlane, creators of the video in a series called "Did You Know? Shift Happens" (see resources), our children of today are learning skills and facts applicable in a world that no longer exists. And in part, this is very true. Consider these facts highlighted in his video and those that run later in the series:

- Both China and India have more Honors kids than America has kids.
- The top 10 "in demand" jobs in 2013 did not exist in 2004.
- The U.S. Department of Labor estimates that by the time a child in today's world turns 38, they will have held 10-14 different jobs.
- Facebook is available in more than 70 languages.
- Google had approximately 2.7 billion searches conducted in the year 2006. In 2012, that number became 31 billion searches in **one month**. And in 2013, it rose again to a staggering 100 billion searches a month.
- The amount of technical information is doubling every two years; so much that the knowledge acquired by a student entering college today will be 50% outdated by the third year in college.
- One week of information provided in *The New York Times* is more than a person would have encountered during a lifetime in the 18th century.

Do you know what a zettabyte is? It's 10^{21} bytes. It is estimated that the World Wide Web reached 4 zettabytes in 2013 (Currier, 2013). Still feel like they are growing up in the same world you did?

Believe it or not, there is a research group that carefully monitors the characteristics of and success rates of incoming college freshmen all across America. The CIRP at the Higher Educational Research Institute at UCLA conducts a very lengthy and thorough survey of these students to keep a pulse on how our educational system is doing. By thorough I mean that the 2012 version of the survey included over 192,900 students entering 283 colleges in the United States. That's thorough. And findings indicate that 84.3% of those freshmen entering college believe they will graduate in four years. On average, however, only 40.6% of those students actually do. Another 15.8% complete their undergraduate work in five years, with 4.5% finishing in six years. That's a total of just over 60% (60.9% to be exact). Of course, this means that 40% of freshmen entering college still take longer than six years to complete their Bachelor's degree...if they do at all. That's a statistic that should definitely concern parents who are paying hefty tuition bills! But for an educator, those are just surface ripples indicating an approaching storm. To use an old saying, "The devil is in the details."

When we talk about "college-readiness", the problem of making sure our students have the knowledge and skills to navigate a world that doesn't even exist yet is a very daunting task. But even if we just look at today, the news is still murky, at best. Only 81.1% of college freshmen in 2012 completed a Pre-Calculus or Trigonometry course before going off to college. That means that almost 20% did not...or one in five. And only 29.4% of those same freshmen had a high school course in Probability and Statistics. We have to be mathematically savvy here...because the NCES (National Center for Education Statistics) reports that in 2009, only 11% of high school students took a course in Probability and Statistics. That means that the larger number for college freshmen is attributed to the fact that those students going into college after high school have different backgrounds than those who aren't even making it to a campus the next Fall. The NCES also reports that only 68% of students graduating high school had BOTH a Biology and Chemistry course. So, 23% of our high school graduates don't even have a minimal balance of physical science and life science in their background. How are we going to build the STEM curriculum and develop more highly qualified engineers, medical professionals, and technology specialists with those kinds of numbers? And more importantly, why are these concerns being raised in this guidebook? Because parents have a positive influence on not only the courses their teenagers select in high school...but also whether they are allowed to drop those courses during the semester just because "the course is really hard". Yes...and so is life. Much harder, in fact, if you are not prepared for it. And, if focusing on the skill attainment itself is not reason enough to make sure our teenagers have wise course selections in high school, we should consider that current ranges between 20% and 40% of all college freshmen have to take at least one remedial course in college before they can progress to the primary level coursework accepted for credit at many institutions. In other words, they are having to correct for a knowledge and skill deficit that actually developed before they even walked onto campus.

~ Day 16 ~

WHEN TO GRAB THE LIFE JACKET

I can still vividly remember taking my son to swimming lessons. I hated those moments. Not because of anything involving him, but the fact that I had to watch from the sidelines as the instructor tried to get him to first hold his breath, then swim away from the side of the pool, and finally to dive on his own. Each time, I could read the terror in my child's face, which was probably matched by...and reflecting...my own fear. It was definitely one of those events when I was more than willing to just jump in and do the task myself to spare my child the trepidation. But because I refrained from intervening, he is now quite an avid swimmer. What is the lesson I learned? I should have let his father take him.

From a teacher's viewpoint, it is never a question of whether a performance or grade in a class will be less than desirable based on the student's or the parent's standards...but only when. None of us are perfect. And, even though we are very reliable in behavior, there will be numerous factors that affect our performance from time to time. This is especially true in the classroom. As a parent and considering communication technology as it has developed in today's society, it is all-to-easy to send a quick e-mail to the teacher at the first sign of distress in the grade. However, there are a few things to consider when taking a moment to align our actions with the long-term desired outcomes we are trying to achieve.

First, if the child is in middle or high school, it is strongly recommended that the student actually be the one to make the initial e-mail contact with the teacher. This does NOT mean that teachers do not want to hear from parents, or that we shouldn't hear from them. This is about allowing the student an opportunity to gain the autonomy and efficacy we have already introduced earlier in the guidebook. In this way, if a concern arises later and a "life jacket" is needed...we already have it in place. I would even recommend that the parent be in the room and looking over the shoulder of the child as they compose their letter. Then, if you have genuine concerns about follow through, you can step in at any time, but have not done so before your teenager had practice at problem-solving skills. What an opportunity to work on writing etiquette, communication skills, conflict resolution, and building self-reliance all at the same time! Then, when the teacher responds, take the opportunity to read the return e-mail along with your teen. Begin a dialog with your teenager on how to proceed. Sometimes this means that the student needs to set up a time to visit the teacher after school for additional help. Other times the clarification in an e-mail is enough to gather details on an assignment and complete the work at home.

The more your child gains comfort in directly corresponding with the teacher, the better. In fact, for any students, it would be ideal to simply send an initial e-mail at the beginning of a course just to say hello to the teacher and to begin the communications on a positive note. Sometimes students just send a link to something they found pertinent to class discussion that day. Many times they just have a question or two related to the current class activities. Either way, it is always beneficial for the child to initiate this link, and allows the teacher to place a face with a name and a subsequent e-mail connection in the first few weeks of school. It is good to keep in mind that this form of communication is not texting, thus expecting an immediate response would be beyond the abilities of a teacher who is in the classroom all day. Give the teachers 24 hours to have a full cycle of their daily schedule (including any planning time) to read and respond to all the communications coming in from many students, other teachers, administrators, and so on.

So, for the activity today, your teenager should send out an initial e-mail contact with each of her teachers. This will make it much more likely that she will make the contact again later in the year if a concern arises, and a resolution can be easily obtained. Besides, when are we *really* told to put on our life jackets? When entering the boat, not after we have sprung a leak!

INITIAL TEACHER CONTACT LOG

List of Teachers to E-mail (include address):   Date Sent: Date Reply Received:

_____   _____   _____

_____   _____   _____

_____   _____   _____

_____   _____   _____

_____   _____   _____

_____   _____   _____

_____   _____   _____

List of Teacher Websites or Electronic Schedule / Assignment Posting Platforms:

_____

_____

_____

_____

_____

_____

_____

_____

Specific Notes From Correspondence:

~ Day 17 ~

THE PLIMSOLL LINE

Named after a British merchant and member of Parliament in the 1800s, the Plimsoll line is the mark we frequently see on the hull of a ship that looks like a series of horizontal hash marks. In the early days of trade, the shipping companies were notorious for overloading the boats with as much cargo as they could carry, and then some. As a result, many ships running into rough weather would ended up capsizing, with the cargo and the entire crew lost. Samuel Plimsoll wanted a standard marker on the ships that would indicate warning if they were loaded too heavily and sitting too low in the water. Teachers see this same effect in students who get weighted down with numerous projects all due at the same time, or homework from different teachers with staggered due-dates. Before you know it, the student is sinking with the perception that there is too much to do and not enough time to do it. In most cases, the teen in this situation is lacking a Plimsoll line to indicate how much of a load to take-on, and how to handle that load.

Organization is one of the greatest skills any person can have, and the one that is frequently most lacking in teenagers. Recall from earlier sections in the guidebook that the pre-frontal cortex of a teenager's brain is rapidly blossoming with new dendritic connections, but not really filtering or problem-solving at the necessary level for academic success during these years. In fact, you probably see many signs of this at home, too. And, not just in the forgetfulness that accompanies this age. If you ask a teenager to get the newspaper on the driveway, then go outside and move the patio furniture into the garage, and finally turn-on the yard sprinkler, you might see an order of events that is something other than what you expected. First, the teen turns-on the sprinkler, thus soaking the patio furniture. Then, he returns outside, only to bring dripping wet patio furniture into the garage. And finally, comes to you saying, "Do you really want the newspaper...because it's all wet." What was missed here? Given that moments like these tend to characterize every family that has a teenager, it will come as no surprise that the part of the brain responsible for not only coordinating movements of the body, but also coordinating organizational skills is not yet mature at this phase. The cerebellum, located in the back of the cranial region, is one of the areas of the brain that makes processing tasks a little smoother, especially when it involves a series of tasks.

Since organizational skills are at a deficit at this age, and the demand to build them in high school is at an all-time premium, what we really need are some scaffolding supports that will enable the adolescent to go outside the self for these tools until they become internal skills later in college. Many schools utilize class notebook organizers that are paper hard-copies printed by the schools and supplied to the students. This is a terrific method, and one that can also organize the teachers so that all members of the faculty are using the same method. This increases predictability for the student and ease of transition from one class to another.

However, with technology today there are numerous organizational apps offered in social media that are sometimes preferred by many students over the hard-copy paper versions provided by the school. In part, this is because students almost always have their cell phones with them. And because today's student has grown-up in this advanced society, they are more familiar with the platforms on which these apps are generated. If your child uses the school version, that is terrific. But if your teen prefers an electronic organizer, the activity today is to find one that fits the needs of your teenager and upload it to his/her phone. But there is an additional part to the activity. Those students who have organizational difficulties frequently forget to log the assignments while in class, or they get home and don't access the information. If a parent provides the initial motivation and direction to actually check the organizer on Fridays before social events of the weekend take place with peers, then the incentive to actually use the device comes full circle. This action usually closes the gap on communications between home and school, materials needed for homework, and knowing due dates so that time management can be at a premium. However, the key component here is consistency in checking the organizer once a week, and including a link between the incentive to do so and something that motivates your teen to accomplish these tasks.

List of Organizational Apps

This is by no means an exhaustive list of organizational apps. The author does not recommend nor endorse any specific application, but merely the use of any organizer that works for your teenager. Because of the nature of apps with updates and alterations, keep in mind that these apps will most likely change in some content and delivery that is not known or monitored by the author of this guidebook.

Notability	To Do Matrix
Evernote	Beep Me
Awesome Note	Complete Class Organizer
Google Calendar	FC Tasks
Studious	Sticky Notes for iPad
Remember the Milk	iHomework

~ Day 18 ~

SIGHTING AN ALBATROSS

In the poem, *The Rime of the Ancient Mariner"* by Samuel Taylor Coleridge, the mariner gets "a little nervous" as he sails for days but cannot find land. He sees an albatross circling above the ship, which is good luck. But in his confusion and frustration, he uses his crossbow to shoot the bird that has been hovering and pestering him. He later finds out the significance of the albatross...when the other sailors get angry at him for killing a good luck charm ...and they proceed to hang the dead bird around his neck. Sailors are known for being very superstitious, which is actually an indication of having an external locus of control.

Locus of control (briefly mentioned in an earlier chapter) is a psychological trait that indicates whether a person feels that they are in control of their own actions and destiny, or whether external factors are determining their outcomes in life. A person with an internal locus of control feels that they have control over their own actions and that those actions determine outcomes in their lives. Individuals with an external locus of control feel that their own behaviors don't have much of an effect (if any) influencing the circumstances that develop in their lives and the results are beyond their control. It's understandable that sailors in the early days didn't think they had much control over whether they made it to the other shore, or avoiding a sinking ship. With little knowledge of ocean currents, storm patterns, and virtually no technology, they really didn't have much control. But people in all walks of life have a tendency toward one of the two types of loci, not just sailors. And when it comes to students, their locus has a lot of influence on how they handle challenges in their lives. The original scale to measure whether a person is more internally or externally based came about in 1966 by Psychologist Julian Rotter. It is frequently used in the adult world to predict job performance. The one for this guidebook has been modified by the author to specifically address aspects of the adolescent's world.

Locus of Control Scale for Adolescents

This scale was based on the research of other versions, but was designed by the author of this guidebook in order to align the items with those encountered by adolescents. For each item, give a rating of 1 to 5 according to the descriptions below:

1	indicates	"Not true almost all of the time."
2	indicates	"Mostly not true."
3	indicates	"Sometimes true and sometimes false."
4	indicates	"Mostly true."
5	indicates	"True almost all of the time."

1. _____ For the most part, grades reflect the effort you put into the class.
2. _____ I select my elective courses based on what my parents want me to take.
3. _____ I think I can really make a difference in the world if I try.
4. _____ There are some subjects I just don't do well in no matter how hard I try.
5. _____ Some studying strategies are more effective for me than other ones.
6. _____ Social activities and extracurricular activities affect my grades.
7. _____ I think a lot before I make major decisions, weighing the choices.
8. _____ If I am tardy to class, it is because of something I couldn't control.
9. _____ I have the ability to keep a good attendance record for myself.
10. _____ Having a study routine doesn't really increase my test scores.
11. _____ I verbally participate in most of my classes.
12. _____ I frequently change my mind about which career interests me.
13. _____ I tend to take more class notes with more detail than some of my peers.
14. _____ How well a student does on tests is mostly about how smart you are.
15. _____ How hard I work in high school can determine which college accepts me.
16. _____ Life is really about a lot of random, chance events that happen to you.
17. _____ I accomplish most of the goals I set for myself.
18. _____ If I get in trouble, it's because I was in the wrong place at the wrong time.
19. _____ You don't have to be popular to be happy.
20. _____ Most people with good jobs are just lucky.

Total the points for all of the odd-numbered questions here: _____
Total the points for all of the even-numbered questions here: _____

Odd-numbered questions indicate an internal locus of control; while even-numbered questions indicate an external locus of control. Those students with a higher score for internal locus of control are more likely to feel they can positively influence their own lives and solve their own problems in life. A score of 35 or higher is considered "strong" in either category.

~ *Day 19* ~
ALL HANDS ON DECK

We would never see a situation in which the captain of a ship, upon realizing that he is headed into a storm, would encourage half the crew to go below deck and take a nap. The same is true for our students. They have allies...many allies. These allies are classmates and they are bonded to each other, not by common fondness for the same music or the same hobbies, nor even previously established friendships...but by the common goal of attaining academic success in the class. When the challenging concepts and projects begin to seep out of the woodwork, this is not a time to retreat into isolation, but rather to find what I refer to as "study buddies".

There are hundreds of variations on the old saying, "Two heads are better than one" for good reason. To have a study buddy in the class means that you now have two perspectives of the learning that is taking place in the class. There are two sets of notes, which can be compared to one another to make sure that nothing was missed on that one day when you had to miss part of class for an orthodontist's appointment. How does a student know if they missed critical notes or a valuable handout if they never see the full load of material? This teacher recommends having a study buddy in each class to all of my students every year. However, most students don't begin to use the method until around October. This is very unfortunate, because by this time, much of the semester grade is already cemented into the gradebook, and the student doesn't have time or means to go back and learn the old concepts while they are still trying to understand second quarter material.

Once in a while, I will hear either a student or parent respond with, "She likes to study by herself", meaning they aren't going to take the advice. This is their choosing, however the two types of studying are not mutually exclusive of one another. A student can spend a limited amount of time studying with peers, and then return home to study alone or do so the next evening. It's not a coincidence that college towns always have a large number of coffee houses with study areas. College students have figured out the power in numbers. And, what the teacher explains in one or two ways in class is a different approach then the approach a peer will take in explaining the same concept. Quite frequently, because teenagers think more similarly, a student having a tough time understanding a concept will finally overcome the hurdle when a classmate explains it. This is why peer tutoring is so effective in many programs. And, while it is admirable that parents try to assist in studying with their children, by the time they are in upper middle school and high school, much of the material is so specific that unless your job is in the exact same field, it is hard to recall just how to calculate the moles of a substance based on the grams and chemical formula or composition. Often times a parent trying to help their teenager study can get very frustrated when they don't know how the teacher presented the methods or in what context. But of course, they don't know. They weren't in class. The classmates, however, were there. And they DID receive the exact same instruction on the exact same day in the exact same context.

An added benefit to working with a study buddy is that, if they are invited over to your house to study, you can learn a lot more about the class via discussions between the students. You may even get to see how the other student organizes her notes, and most importantly, how your child's note-taking skills compare to those of his/her peers. This is a tremendous opportunity on many levels, for both you and your teenager. Today, ask your teen to identify someone who can be a potential "study buddy" in each of her classes. The phone number or s-mail address of the classmate should also be listed and ready...before issues come up in the class. If your teen is new to the school or just shy, saying "I don't know anyone in that class" is NOT an excuse. GET to know someone! Get to know several "someones". Preferably, this happens at the beginning of a semester. It sometimes helps to agree on a timeline with your teen on when the list will be completed and ready when needed. If an adolescent is dragging her feet on finding these peers, it is sometimes because they don't want to be seen as "not having mastered the material" by a classmate. But the truth is that no one (other than the teacher) has mastered the material. And last, a very major benefit to having a study buddy is that there is no better motivation in preparing for a test if your peers have a better grasp of the content than you do! Sometimes students say "I know this stuff", that is, until they have a conversation with a classmate who knows a lot more and is more prepared for the test. Now THAT is a very accurate reality check! And, if the study buddy group still has questions after conversing, they can even go in to see the teacher as a group! For some shy students, the strength in numbers is just the combination needed to break the ice and get comfortable with asking the teacher for additional help. As an added note for parents, if you are monitoring the visits your child attends with the teacher, it's always a good idea to ask for validation of the session. For example, ask to see your teen's notebook, which should now have some of the teacher's handwriting added in places that were addressed. You can even require your child to obtain a signature from the teacher verifying the date and time of the extra help sessions. I've seen too many situations in conferences when a parent was told by their child that they had been in to see me frequently...and never did so. The teacher has every motivation to help students after school...that's part of their job. Unfortunately, the student has every motivation to avoid getting help if it means more time with friends and accountability is not an issue.

POTENTIAL STUDY BUDDIES

	Study Buddy	**Contact Info.**
1st class:	_____	_____
2nd class:	_____	_____
3rd class:	_____	_____
4th class:	_____	_____
5th class:	_____	_____
6th class:	_____	_____
7th class:	_____	_____

For each of the "Study Buddies" found above, what are some other extra-curricular activities in which both you and they are commonly involved? Are you both in Band? Are you both members of the Chess club? This provides just one more common tie between the two of you, and another opportunity to connect and talk about class activities. Note these below as well:

Activities:

Beyond Academics

You're probably wondering how I am going to connect the "sailing ship analogy" with activities outside of academics, right? Here goes. Some people are more sensitive to shifts in movement than others, whether riding in a car, enjoying a roller coaster, or on the deck of a ship. Motion sickness, or sea sickness, in this case, is essentially the phenomenon that occurs when your visual cues do not match up with your responses of motion and balance (located in the semicircular canals of your inner ear). The brain is being told by your eyes that you are stationary. But the inner ear is reporting that you are rocking back and forth. The discrepancy of input does not go well with your perceptive abilities...the brain doesn't like to be lied to. This is why seasickness can actually be worse if you go below deck and lie down on a cot or sit at an anchored table with no view of the horizon. Many routine sailors recommend getting on deck with the open air...and watching the horizon. Now your eyes are reporting the same perceptions of movement that your ears are encountering. Here comes the connection. These additional activities are other areas of interest in a teenager's life that round out the facets of our hobbies, activities, and talents, and skills. These are parts of our personality that, while not in the center, are definitely there accentuating the whole of the person and allowing us to branch out our strengths into various regions...just like keeping your eye on the horizon. If you lose sight of it, you may not know if you are upright.

Many therapists recommend having variety in our activities and social connections so that, if we encounter rough waters in one area of our lives, we can gain solid ground and perspective in the other ones that are already a part of our routine. People who are interconnected with other members of society are less likely to feel outcast...or become depressed. Teachers know that students who are involved with their school in ways beyond the classroom tend to be happier and feel they are part of the student body more than those who are isolated and uninvolved. These teenagers also have the added social circles beyond class...the cast of the play, the team, the percussion section of the band, etc. This means more chances to develop friendships...and with people who have more in common than just enjoying the same school subjects. It also means that there are added adult eyes watching out for your child at school and at these events. A coach who knows that one of his baseball players is struggling in math class is more likely to talk with the math teacher, and encourage (often require) the student to go in for extra help. This is especially significant once your teenager advances in grades to where they are rotating teachers within one day, perhaps having as many as seven different classes and seven different teachers. The coach or sponsor of the activity is probably monitoring **ALL** of the grades of his/her players. What an excellent resource for communication...and what an advocate for your child! Now, this does not mean that the author is recommending "the more activities...the better". Certainly **NOT**! Every child has their own preference of activities, and their own limit on hours in the day and energy in the body.

It is not uncommon (especially in more affluent, suburban settings) for teachers to see students who are suffering academically because they are overloaded with too many activities. And, the priority of academics can easily get shuffled down the line. Why? Because the performances in these activities are more...acute. They are fewer and further between than daily school work. Thus, a student (and sometimes a parent) will view the "Friday night game" as taking precedence over the current grade in math. After all, the child will be in this math class all semester. We have plenty of time to pull up the grade, right? But the game against "Rival High" is once a season. This is it...the moment of moments. Math will wait. Of course, here's the flaw in that logic. There's always another game next week, and the week after that, and after that. There's even a season after this one. And, by the time the season is over and the child can now focus undivided attention on understanding math skills, we may be looking at the last few weeks of the semester. Both the skills and knowledge of the class are sequential and build upon one another. What a child doesn't learn in September will definitely affect him in November. Believe it or not, a weak understanding of math in the early years of high school can really affect the student's understanding (and performance) of Chemistry or Physics in the last years of high school. Many students and parents don't apply the same understanding of concept acquisition and linear progression to the sciences and math as they do for, say, reading. If a child was having difficulty reading in the second grade, and the system failed to identify the concern and work on the skills, then that child would be behind in reading and comprehension from that point forward, right? So, it's good for us as both parents and teachers to remind ourselves that the skills are truly what is important. And, both the depth of meaning in attaining true understanding of concepts and the magnification of ripple effects from any gaps in their background abound with every additional skill they attempt to acquire in school beyond that time.

—

~ Day 20 ~

A CURE FOR SEASICKNESS

We all lose our perspective from time to time. And as described earlier, while it may be tempting to go below deck and lie down, the advice continuously given is to get on deck where you can see the horizon line. The more senses involved in observing the actual motion being experienced, the better. This is true with school involvement and students.

For the activity today, let's encourage your teen to become involved in a school activity that is outside the academics of the classroom. The first step is to investigate which ones are available. Some involve try-outs that only occur once a year or at few times scheduled during the year (football, soccer, musicals, etc.). Others are ongoing and may even involve classes in which you need to be enrolled to participate (choir, debate, student council, etc.). But not all activities are like the previous two categories. There are many groups of interest that typically meet after school (chess clubs, science clubs, etc.) and are simply a terrific collection point for those students with similar interests. Have your child connect today with either the main office or the counseling office to ask for a list of these activities. Then, ask your teen to identify two different groups that seem interesting to him. Next, your teen should contact the sponsor each of the group within the next few days to see when the next group gathering occurs. The key here is the initial contact, and to identify at least two or three peers who are already in the group. The sponsor will know student contacts at every grade level, and they are more than eager to increase the numbers of students in their group! Keep in mind that, while it is very tempting as a caring parent to go ahead and make the contact yourself, this would take away an opportunity from your teen to meet the secretary in the office (or counselor), find the sponsor's classroom and meet him/her, and feel a sense of self- advocacy and accomplishment.

Your child needs to build all of these in order to truly feel that s/he's a part of the school and to witness that he really can solve her/his own issues and make social contacts to become part of a larger group. Your support can come in the shape of follow-through in the next few days to see if these contacts actually occurred and the dates for meetings actually placed in your child's planner or calendar. More networking inevitably equals more friends and a feeling of belonging that will buoy your teen through future tough times. This is not only avoiding sea sickness now...this is establishing the horizon line, which is prevention for the future!

Area of Interest #1: _____

Sponsor: _____

Activities and Events: _____

_____

_____

Meeting Times: _____

New Friendships: _____

_____

Area of Interest #2: _____

Sponsor: _____

Activities and Events: _____

_____

_____

Meeting Times: _____

New Friendships: _____

_____

~ Day 21 ~

THE BUOYS MARK THE CHANNEL

Buoys have several purposes. They can be used to indicate an object below, to mark the location of a channel, to signal diver positions, or even for fishing. Some buoys have lights while others have radio signals. Some even give off sonar while others detect sound waves traveling through the water. But they all have one thing in common in addition to floating: they indicate a time to pay attention to the environment.

By nature, teenagers are very self-absorbed and myopic in their view of the world around them. Their brains are very busy working on developing the child into an adult, both cognitively and emotionally. By mid-adolescence, much of the physical growth has already begun and is quite progressed. But the brain will continue to develop through the teen years and into the twenties. In part, this lack of perspective of the world around them can sometimes contribute to the magnification of a small setback in life into what appears to be a major crash. Anxiety and depression are very possible along with social strife due to volatile emotional reactions to events. One way to address the tunnel vision in teenagers is to remind them, not in words but in action, that there is a much bigger world out there. The reality check can come from helping others in need of any number of levels. The experience of observing the struggles of others or other facets of society can be a grounding and humbling moment of growth for a person. And, of course, helping others not only strengthens the community, but allows the individual stepping up to develop efficacy. They begin to see that they actually can change the world, even in small increments over a great length of time. Community service is also known to build resilience in a person's character (Ginsburg, 2011). And, if they can exert a positive influence on the lives of others, then they can definitely do so for their own as well. Select one of the community service ideas below (or one of your own) and contribute along with your teen. The experience will bring you together in many ways beyond those you expect, and the new perspective will provide a new platform for relating to the community and to others.

20 COMMUNITY SERVICE IDEAS

- Gather non-perishable food items at the grocery store to donate
- Donate old clothes to a shelter
- Volunteer time at a soup kitchen or homeless shelter
- Join a social group that is cleaning up litter by roadways
- Buy new toys and blankets for a children's hospital
- Volunteer time at a retirement home
- Offer to do lawn care (mowing, raking leaves) for an elderly neighbor
- Hold a bake sale for a charity
- Sign-up and participate in a charity race
- Volunteer at animal shelters
- Join a mentoring or tutoring group for free
- Collect old paint cans for proper disposal at waste management facilities
- Collect old cell phones for organizations that recycle them
- Volunteer at events to support people with disabilities
- Plant a community garden or trees in a reclamation project
- Volunteer time, effort or goods during a natural disaster
- Become a pen pal for younger children
- Organize supply boxes for military personnel
- Organize a campaign for recycling plastic, glass, aluminum, and paper products
- Adopt an acre of forest, livestock, or an endangered animal online by supporting an international organization

~ *Day 22* ~

MONITORING THE TRIM

This is not in reference to making the boat look aesthetically pleasing. The trimming a boat is a method for balancing the boat on the water, from front to back (bow to stern) and left to right (port to starboard). If the boat isn't balanced, you are in for a rough ride! And the trim, just like your levels of stress, has to be adjusted according to the speed of the boat, the conditions of the water (smooth or choppy), and the amount of weight being carried. For a student, this would mean that one has to pay attention to how urgently they are trying to accomplish everything (due dates, etc.), how many other things are adding stress to one's life (relatives, holidays, major events, friendship drama), and how many other things one is trying to handle at one time.

For parents, an important point to remember is that, while we all have a genetic predisposition to the release and metabolic rate of handling cortisol when it enters the bloodstream in stressful situations, we learn many of our coping mechanisms by modeling. Teenagers will often use the methods they see in their parents. And, if a certain stressor is affecting the entire family (like a relative who is ill, a holiday, moving, changing jobs) then it might be a good idea to do some de-stressing activities together! The following are ideas for today's activity. They are actually based on research about both the physiological and psychological factors of stress. While the activities may seem simple, they actually produce changes in both the physical and emotional balance of the human body. They key is to truly *use* them! And, because every person's background and physical composition is different, what works for one person may not work for another. You have to learn, by experience, which ones are most effective for the outcome you desire for decreasing your own anxiety levels. Any of these should be done for at least 20-40 minutes.

Strategies For Handling Stress

- Take a physical break, removing yourself from the stressor, and do something that makes you laugh.

- Take a break away from the source and listen to music that calms you and refocuses your thoughts away from the stressor.

- Did you know that pets are known to not only reduce stress, but to improve your immune system? Spend 20-40 minutes outside with your pet.

- Drink two full glasses of water, which help to metabolize stress hormones in the blood.

- Play a musical instrument or other talent you have developed that requires the use of skills that combine physical and mental ability.

- Exercise...and this doesn't have to be rigorous! Walk, bike, skate, play racquetball.

- Light candles and take a soothing bath without dwelling on the stressor.

- Don't do things that stress the body...like staying up too late, taking in an additional amount of caffeine than normal, etc.

- Breathing exercises. These actually slow-down and "re-set" the autonomic system.

Reflecting on the Activity:

- What were some of the stressors affecting you?

- Which method(s) did you select?

- Did you find the method(s) to be beneficial in reducing stress and anxiety?

Activities:

Work / Jobs

It is very critical to the development of young adults to develop a sense of both efficacy and autonomy. One of the ways this can be achieved is, of course, by having a job. A job outside of school provides an additional venue in which teens can develop autonomy that is not related to academic achievement.   It can also be an extension of a support system outside the family. Typically, there are people at the job site of varying ages and maturity levels. This provides a great background of diversity for the teenager who is observing adult roles and how to interact with superiors (such as managers and bosses). This is also an environment in which they can achieve competence without competition, which is sometimes present as an unintended factor in the school setting. Additionally, the adolescent will gain a new set of skills and background knowledge that can be applied in college and later in a major career. However, there are many caveats that should be considered before selecting *which* job might be most beneficial. And, what serves as the best answer for one child will not be the same for another.

The number of hours a teenager works needs to be carefully weighed against the amount of time needed for school work and other extra-curricular activities. Prioritization is one of the most important features not only for attaining success in all of these areas, but in limiting the amount of stress and anxiety that is encountered during these adolescent years. Any boss who truly cares about your long-term success should be supportive of your priorities and dedication to your academic development and your other commitments.

~ *Day 23* ~
THE MAST AND THE SAIL

When you look on the horizon, usually the first part of a ship that you see is the mast. If the sails are up, they look like one fused object. In many ways, they are. Without one, the other cannot function. As teachers, we have observed countless times that those students who have a goal or a dream are the ones who have a path. The ones we tend to worry about are those with no direction; because this translates bi-directionally with no motivation. If we trace the path in reverse, a career goal helps to focus both college and major choices, which then help to maintain high school course selections and solid grades (Harackiewicz , 2002).

Ask your child to make a list of about three different careers in which they are currently interested. Then for today's activity, ask your child to go online and to do a phone interview with someone in this field to find out the answers to the questions (next page) for each of the careers. It is very critical that your child specifically finds out what type of degree (including majors) is required for these careers. And, in order to really update yourself on which type of degree is being *hired* for these jobs, don't hesitate to call businesses directly and inquire about skills and areas of concentration.

It is overwhelming to think today's student will have 10-14 jobs by the age of 38 (Fisch, 2013). Tomorrow's workforce has to be more adaptable and have more transient skills than any preceding generation. The information brought forward in technology today is developing so rapidly that the educational system is having trouble keeping up with the demand...not of workers, but of the types of skills that will be needed. Yes, teenagers will be very hesitant to make the actual connections with adults in these fields. But this skill is essential for success later in college and in their own career! After your teen completes the task, sit down and discuss how your child feels about the information obtained. If your teenager finds a clarified interest in one particular career, consider setting a day (within a week so that both your memories are fresh from the initial conversation) to ask a person in the field to allow your child to "shadow" them for a few hours (at a time that is not intrusive with school work).

CAREER EXPLORATION

1. What is involved during a typical day in this profession?

2. Which courses in high school help to prepare a person for this field of study?

3. Which degrees or licensures/certifications are required for this profession?

4. Describe a few personality traits that are beneficial to have if one pursues this career.

5. Describe a few personality traits that would make it difficult to succeed in this career.

6. How is this career field valuable to society in general?

7. What are the current employment trends/demands for this job?

8. What are the most rewarding factors about this job?

9. What are some of the most challenging factors in this job?

10. What is the most valuable piece of advice you (person in the field) can give to me if I went into this same profession?

~ Day 24 ~

THE WINDS AND CURRENTS OF MOTION

Now that your child has identified (and possibly had to modify their list based on what they learned about various careers) areas of interest on day 23, let's back up and ask your teen to now do a search (internet again) for about five or six different colleges or universities they are interested in attending after high school. If a technical school is required for these jobs sets, do the same for these careers.

The activity for today is in searching specifically for the course requirements of the degree being sought after that will prepare your child for a career in their field of interest. Refer to Appendix D for this activity. Notice that one question specifically asks for the minimum GPA or ACT/SAT score required for admission into the program. This particular question is usually a real eye-opener. Even after I have spoken to students about minimum GPAs for admission, they just don't take it "close to home" until they read it on the university website. And, they need to know the difference between the GPA that will get them onto the campus of their choice, and the GPA that will get them into the program within the specific college (such as engineering, law, business, education, etc.). Typically, the GPA for admission into the specific school or college during the junior or senior year is higher than the general admission one for entering freshmen. I have found that some of my students think they can just "coast" once they are admitted to a university. Nothing is further from the truth. This is a good time to introduce the term "perpetual sophomore" and how you never want to be one. Most of the questions offered here can be answered online, but some can and should be answered directly (by email, phone, visit) by an authority at the campus. Have your teenager discover the answers to all 25 questions for each of the three colleges/universities, and then triangulate the information for a discussion.

COLLEGE CLIMATE

1. Geographical location of college/university: _____

2. Annual tuition and books: _____

3. Housing Options and Costs: _____

4. Scholarships / Financial Aid awarded? _____

5. Minimum GPA and High School Prerequisites: _____

6. ACT or SAT scores needed for admission to programs? _____

7. Number of students living on campus: _____

8. Number of students in freshman class: _____

9. Failure/Success rate after first year: _____

10. What percent of freshmen return for sophomore year? _____

11. Are there work-study opportunities? _____

12. What is the average size of introductory classes? _____

13. What is the four-year graduation rate? _____

14. What types of tutoring/support programs are offered? _____

15. When do campus visits occur? _____

16. What clubs or activities do you have on campus? _____

17. Could you send me one copy of your campus newspaper? _____

18. What is the crime rate on campus? _____

19. Which three programs or majors have highest enrollment your college? _____

20. Which three programs or majors is your college most known for? _____

21. Does your university accept Advanced Placement credit for certain courses? ____

22. What is campus security like at your university? _____

23. What does your college offer than others do not? _____

24. What is the placement rate for graduates? _____

25. What is the technology like on your campus? _____

~ Day 25 ~

USING A SEXTANT

A sextant is a very fascinating piece of equipment dating all the way back to the mid-1700s. They are designed to calculate the angle between a celestial object and the horizon, thereby providing the location of the ship. It's a clever frame of reference. And, that is exactly what we need for young adults who, for the first time in their lives, are beginning to make their own decisions about course selections in high school. Indeed, it's probably the first time different courses were offered, which also means that decisions could be made that are not in the best interest of where we want to be at the end of our high school journey. For example, if a student wants to be an Engineer, then taking Basket Weaving I, II, and III will probably not adequately prepare her for a major in Aerospace Engineering. The problem is, s/he won't realize s/he is lacking the appropriate skills until the time of actually being on campus and attempting to take all of the Math and Physics required for the major. And, unless a parent, counselor, or teacher advises her carefully, the temptation to take an easy course for an easy grade is frequently too hard to resist for the senior facing high school burn-out. By the way, back in the 70s, we actually could take classes on macramé. Of course, I use that skill frequently when researching or making lesson plans. Many school systems didn't have curriculum designers back then. But I can still weave a plant holder.

For day 25, you are asked once again to send your teenager out scavenging for supplies. This time, she needs to go online or contact the college of her choice directly and find the exact listing of required courses and electives needed to earn the degree she seeks. However, she should also look up these listings for the other two college choices from the previous activity on day 24. Then she will be able to analyze the lists and see how the university requirements differ from one another for this particular major. She will also begin to see the horizon of what is to come for day 26...which is the question high school teachers and counselors deal with quite often among our juniors and seniors: "Which skills and background knowledge do I need to be successful in these college courses?"

What we find is that in acquiring the knowledge of what is needed from a third party (not parents and not your high school), teenagers begin to award a great deal of validity to the reality of prerequisites and requirements for degrees. When high school students realize that they will (depending on the university) most likely be required to take one class of introductory science even if they are majoring in areas that seem very distant from science (like Fine Arts), they suddenly become more motivated to focus on the content of what they are learning in high school. This includes beginning to put the grade earned in perspective. It is a relief for an educator to actually hear seniors having conversations with their peers and teachers about whether they actually know the material, shifting away from the superficial letter grade. In this case, the stars and the horizon that guide them are right in their hands if they do the homework and find the requirements at the next level of study. Notice that the exercise also asks the teenager to investigate minimum GPAs and entrance exams to get into the specific school of study. In yesterday's activity, students had to find the minimum GPA for admission to the college or university. Now they are narrowing-in and looking at the major; which also has admission tests. Many times they think that their high school final exams will be the last tests they ever take in life. That would be nice.

Once your teenager has finished the task, you are encouraged to sit with them and discuss their findings.

MAJOR CONSTELLATIONS

Intended Major: _____

GPA Required for Admission to Specific School of Study: _____

Entrance Exams Required for Admission to School of Study: _____

Intended minor: _____

Required Courses for Major: _____

_____

_____

_____

_____

Prerequisites for Courses:_____

_____

Required Courses for minor: _____

_____

_____

_____

_____

Electives that could be used: _____

_____

_____

_____

_____

~ Day 26 ~
A SAILOR'S KNOT

This activity is a more challenging one than the last two days, because it requires a paradigm shift from GPA requirements and course requirements to the comprehension of both knowledge and skills to be successful in college courses. This is also a great time to introduce the concept of "prerequisites". I have observed that the last decade has produced an increase in people, students and parents alike, who are under the false assumption that just because you can manipulate some educational systems and push your way into a course, the student is then guaranteed success and mastery of the material in the next higher course level. These are frequently the same parents that we hear from in the last week of school who are upset with the teacher because their child struggled, and the end grade is not what they wanted. Passing Algebra with an A means you can definitely handle the basic equations in Chemistry. Passing Algebra with a grade of a D or even a C- means there will be struggles in understanding the equations and applying them in Chemistry. Somewhere, someone has to take up the slack in understanding the material and being prepared for the learning that will occur at the next level. And, that cannot be accomplished by anyone other than the student. Parents can insist that students traverse through their coursework at a pace that is faster than the rate of skill acquisition for their child, but only for so long (and usually only a semester or two). Eventually, the required tasks will surpass the abilities of the student, and failure is imminent. **NO** parent and **NO** teacher ever wants to see this occur.

The activity for today is to actually work backwards. Sitting down with your teen, look again at the information you now have about careers, colleges, and course requirements for majors. This activity will also require the course guidebook for your school or district. Now that we know which courses will be needed for your teen to catch her dream degree and career, make a plan of the courses in high school that will offer the opportunity to learn these skills in preparation for later success. Keep in mind all school or district requirements to graduate!

Another point to consider if your child is considering a competitive major and/or university would be the question of Advanced Placement courses or other versions of college credit courses. The ultimate authority on which courses are allowed for credit or how the credit will be applied in the program (toward requirements or electives) is determined solely by the university. Thus, it is imperative that students check with the college and obtain a clear delineation of these guidelines in writing. Many students who are in a competitive position or a challenging major will elect to take these more rigorous courses in high school. This action is to be highly commended, as it is one of the best ways to truly prepare for college coursework in advance of actually being on campus (when students are also distracted by social lives and how to do their laundry). However, loading up on so many advanced courses that the stress level is overwhelming (and negatively impacting learning the skills) can actually be damaging in the long run. Select the advanced courses that are directly aligned with your chosen major field. Then, if you have time in the schedule for others, consider them carefully without overloading into a compromising situation.

For an AP teacher, it is very sad to see a student who is overwhelmed simply because they are taking too many advanced courses. A general rule of thumb is that an AP course will require an additional hour of work outside of class time for every hour that the class actually meets. So when some students actually attempt to take three AP courses at one time, and they are in roughly six classes a day, even with NO homework in the other three classes, the student will likely need six hours that night to keep pace! Adding in any other work, chores, eating dinner, and any extra-curricular activities (soccer, band, debate, etc. allows for little wiggle room!

Another point that teachers want to avoid is that in which the student loses efficacy or volition when trying to accomplish the challenging tasks in the course. Typically, once the crashing waves hit, the student begins to interpret their struggles as "maybe I can't be successful in this field", when actually that may not be the case at all! The real issue is, once the teen has convinced him/herself that they are helpless and the material in the class is beyond their abilities, there is frequently no going back and convincing him/her otherwise. Give your child the room s/he needs to succeed.

PLOTTING A COURSE IN HIGH SCHOOL

(Your school may actually have a course planning sheet for students. If that is the case, it is recommended that you use the one **they** work from rather than an unfamiliar one.)

English Requirements:

Math Requirements:

Science Requirements:

World Language:

Technology:

Arts:

Courses in student's area for future major:

Electives:

* An important note regarding Advanced Placement courses:

Only the university granting credit can indicate what scores are needed to earn credit, and how it will be applied.

~ Day 27 ~

THE SKILLS OF SAILING

If one of the sailors aboard a ship wants to eventually be the navigator, then learning how to read maps and chart courses would be a good idea while he is attending to his current chores on deck. And, even if he finds, in calculating the courses, that he actually does NOT like the roles involved in being a navigator, this was still time and effort well spent. Now he knows what he doesn't want to do, and didn't waste energy going down a path not suited to his skills.

According to data taken by the Center for Institutional Evaluation, Research and Planning with students from the University of Texas, 21% of freshmen change their majors in the first year of college. For sophomores and juniors, the number is just over 15% (in each year), and even seniors have uncertainty with over 8% shifting goals at the last minute. No parent wants to hear this, especially when they are signing the check for tuition. Overall, the average number of major changes for each college student is three times during their academic years at college.

In part, this is due to the fact that they are still doing a lot of growing and changing psychologically and emotionally. Priorities are shifting, and so is the world around them. A job that may have been in high demand when they were dreaming of careers in middle school may have already shifted to having an excess of graduates struggling to find work. Even once students graduate with a Bachelor's degree, if it is in the business arena, most have to go through an internship with companies before they are actually offered a job. The skills required today are so specific to each and every job, that the companies have the need to conduct additional training that is tailored to their demands in the world of production and sales. Thus, when teenagers are seeking jobs, why not look for ones that are aligned with current interests later career goals? Even summer internships provide a great source of experience, contacts for references, and strengthen any resume.

Selecting a Job

Today's activity is a guide for selecting a job that will extend one's education and skills toward their goal.

1. First, list the elective courses you have taken or will take before you graduate from high school.

2. Then, list the skills you have acquired outside of school that would be helpful to yourself and an employer. Are you trained in using Excel? Do you know how to use tools? Do you have a background in apps for finance? Have you ever created a work schedule for other workers? Do you know how to conduct an inventory? Think of things you can do that some of your friends do NOT know how to do. That will help focus the list to those things that make you unique and more valuable than the collective group of people pursuing the same job.

3. Next, contact a person in this field (hopefully the same field that you are interested in for a later career), and ask if you can actually job shadow the person for a day or two (or more, if possible). As you observe with this person, take note of new skills you are learning, and ask him/her if you can use them as a reference. Then, add this experience to your resume!

4. Make a contact with someone who already works at the company. Get to know this person, and use the network you have developed as a point of conversation in later interviews.

5. Now is the time to actually look for employment in this field. Remember to always show appreciation for the interviewer's time, dress "better" than the typical worker already on the job, present your resume (and portfolio if applicable) along with your application, and always follow-up the next day with a thank you e-mail (this also keeps your name in the person's mind after the interview is over).

6. Remember that perseverance is frequently what lands the job, so don't give up!

7. Never forget the big picture...ultimately your education is what will carry you into college or technical school, so don't take-on so many hours working that you end up compromising your educational achievements at school!

8. Remember that having a job is another way to build your efficacy and autonomy, and adds another branch of social connections that can help you to remain buoyant when things are tough at home or at school.

Activities:

School / Homework

College readiness is a critical concern in America's educational system today. The gap in skills required to be successful in college and the acquired skills developed in high school is increasing, and some would say exponentially. This is because college readiness not only involves academic knowledge and skills, but emotional maturity. A recent survey in 2013 of over 200 college counseling centers representing almost two million college students found that one in ten college students sought campus counseling assistance in one academic year (Munsey, 2010). This is the highest proportion ever seen since data has been collected on the topic. In addition, the problems identified with these students are becoming more severe than what was seen in the past. Some of the higher frequency issues include depression, anxiety, and self-hurting behaviors. Within the group of directors, 73% reported increases in the numbers of acute crises that required immediate response from professionals. Over 90% of the centers had an average of nine students per year that required hospitalization (this is almost 2 students per 1,000 total students on campus). In addition, 60% of the directors indicated a marked increase in the numbers of students with learning disabilities who find the need to visit the centers as well. Most alarming is the report that 80% of those students who actually committed suicide in the academic year surveyed did NOT even seek counseling center assistance! (Gallagher, 2013). We may be sending them to college...but are they ready? And if not, **_why_** not? Where is the system falling down in helping these adolescents to develop coping strategies and resilience?

~ *Day 28* ~

WHO'S STEERING THIS SHIP?!?

For all my years of teaching in various schools and districts, it amazes me that educational systems have not adopted a Parent-Teacher conference system at the high school level that **requires** the student also be in attendance. Now, this is not necessarily what this author advocates for middle and elementary level settings, but definitely for the upper level adolescence who are about to embark on their own adult lives. Because this may not be expected in the school your child attends, I would definitely check with the teacher of the classroom first. It is critical that all members in a conference feel secure about the setting if positive outcomes are to be achieved. Consider that all of the concerns of academic performance at this level are almost completely in the hands of the student, it is stifling to think that the only person who is characteristically absent from these events...is one and the same. No wonder many parents feel frustrated that attending the conference did not provide as much positive movement as they had hoped for.

The activity for today includes a template for the parents and student to use when attending a conference. It is highly recommended that the student is actually the one having the primary discussion with the teacher, with parents sitting in as "observers" who can interject ideas and opinions in a peripheral manner. This is like teaching your child how to drive. You want her to be able to carry these conversations with professors and bosses in the very near future. This is when we begin to build those skills!

It's also good to remember two important things that can easily be forgotten in the moment of dialogue. First, the teacher has the same goals as the family...success for the student. The teacher, contrasted with the parents, will be very objective about the situation. Recall that most high school teachers will have multiple classes with a total load of many students. They aren't taking things...or delivering information...on a personal level. They are professionals, and work with more situations in a given year than you can ever imagine! When parents expect the teacher to be as emotionally invested as the parent, they are bound to perceive the teacher as "falling short" on dedication, when indeed, this is not the case. You would not want a teacher who uses her emotions as primary guidance in the classroom! From the teacher's perspective, the child is either succeeding or is not. And, this does not mean that the teacher doesn't care. They truly do. They wouldn't still be in the classroom otherwise. They just don't exercise character judgments on students based on performance. And this is a very, very good thing! Second, the student needs to take the initiative for follow-up and follow-through. Set a time with your child about two weeks *after* the conference when you can sit down with him/her and revisit the grade, how it has changed, and how the interventions or recommendations generated in the conference have worked.

Before ever going in to the conference, ask your teen these questions about any courses of concern:

Current Grade in Course of Concern: _____

Goal Grade (of student, not parent): _____

Have you already seen the teacher? _____

Which strategies have you used? _____

CONFERENCE TEMPLATE

Before going to the conference, be sure to go online and print the most recent grades (each district has their own version of this). And, have you contacted the teacher to see if your teen can attend the conference? Notice the questions are phrased for the student to ask them...not the parent.

1. Rather than ask the average of grades in a class, ask how your performance ranks compared to other students. Are you generally in the top quarter? The bottom quarter? Or, out of 30 students who took a specific test, where did you rank? There's a lot of information in knowing that you earned the third highest score in the class...or that only two students scored lower than you. See the difference? Let's say you scored 72 out of 100, and you are feeling that you know the material pretty well....but then find out that only two students scored lower than you. Twenty-eight students are performing at a level that is higher than you. This means you have some work to do! Or, if you earned an 88 out of 100, and you are frustrated that your score was not an A...but find that only two students scored higher than you, then that was probably tough material! You actually held your own quite well during a challenging unit.

2. Ask about how the teacher communicates due dates and assignment details to the students. Does she have a website? You could be checking this daily! Does she list the day's lesson on the board? Do you then write them down in your planner?

3. When is the teacher available for students to receive extra help or clarification on work? If you are already challenged in a course, and have not yet visited the teacher for assistance, then guess who is dropping the ball? Remember, you should care more about your learning and your grade than the teacher.

4. What are my greatest strengths in your class?

5. Which skills could I improve?

6. Could you give me some tips on how to organize my notes for your class?

7. Can we make a written plan of action for me to achieve success in class?

8. Is there any material or resource outside of class that might help me as well?

9. Which learning strategies are best matched to the types of assessments in your class?

10. Be sure to share your own class goals, career dreams, and school activities in which you participate with your teacher. They should know these things to better address your needs and to help you succeed.

~ Day 29~
RETURNING TO HARBOR

Returning our focus again to the ultimate goal of raising happy, productive teenagers and launching them successfully into the adult world, it would be good to reflect one last time on building autonomy. This time, we want to focus on those habits that can be influenced at home and carried through to the college campus and directly impact success after high school graduation. In 2010 the Kaiser Family Foundation conducted a very lengthy and detailed survey of teenagers and the use of media in their lives. The study questioned over 2,000 pre-teens and teenagers across the United States. This was actually the third time for this study, which was also taken in 1999 and 2004, which means that the researchers now have data on *changes* in media use over a decade! The researchers found that 71% of teenagers had a TV in their bedroom in 2009...which was up 6% from a decade earlier. In addition, 36% of teens surveyed had a computer in their bedroom...up 15% from 1999. And most alarming, 50% of teenagers had a video game console in their bedroom...up 5% from ten years ago. I say that the last figure is most alarming not because of the percent of increase over ten years, but because (from the perspective of an educator) I can only partially justify having a TV or a computer in the bedroom to keep informed of local and world events, or to do homework. A video game does neither. Thus, the teenager's bedroom has become so trafficked with technology, that there is little in it to influence a good night's sleep.

There are also some concerning trends that can be coupled with those involving media location and use in the home. Primate groups have specific numbers of individuals in them due to an interaction ratio. Once the troops get to a certain size, they tend to splinter off into two groups. This is also true of humans, which have a critical threshold of about 150 people in a group. Once we exceed this number, we tend to feel that the quality of the interactions is so compromised and the efficiency of the group is decreased to the point that forming a second group would be most beneficial socially and psychologically...for the group as well as the individuals within the group (Cohen, 2013). Given that many teenagers today use social media to connect to their peers, many researchers are now addressing the question of whether individuals actually have more loneliness with greater use of the internet and other forms of communication through technology, rather than face-to-face interactions. I've heard many adults in my generation reflecting a concern that "friends" on Facebook are not really friends, and that teenagers today may be developing a misunderstanding that connection is true conversation. Indeed, it is not. And many of our teenagers are so engaged in this method of communication that they even answer electronic modes of communication (texts, cell phone calls, emails) after they have gone to bed for the night! If the tone indicating they have a message sounds, they get out of bed and answer it. Many teenagers actually sleep with their cell phone near their pillow! Thus, we are also looking at the compounding factor of lack of sleep. But not just lack of sleep, sleep interrupted by empty communications, some of which can even be emotionally stirring news or even forms of cyber-bullying. In those cases, now we are dealing with lack of personal connection, lack of sleep, stress increases, and anxiety. Of teenagers producing more than 120 texts per day, more than 60% of these adolescents sleep less than seven hours a night (McLeod, 2011). In actuality, teenagers should be getting closer to just over nine hours based on their metabolism and physical needs according to the National Sleep Foundation. And to make the circle complete, sleep deprivation also elevates cortisol levels in the brain, moving us closer to the tipping point with stress and anxiety (Walsh, 2004).

So, the challenge for today's activity is a big one, but possibly one that will have a tremendous impact on habits our teenagers carry into college if they can connect the positive effects to their success and happiness. For educators, we refer to this as a scaffolding technique for success. The activity is to completely remove the cell phone from a set time at night until a set time in the morning, not just "turned-off" but still in the possession of your teenager. This will involve actually having the cell phone in the possession of the parent. This will be analogous to being on the boat and away from all the commotion on shore. You can finally hear the waves without interference. Perhaps you even notice some seagulls overhead or a school of fish beside the boat...things you never would have observed if you remained at port. You can actually get some rest on deck. And for your teenager, we can now address at least one major variable that may be adversely affecting time and quality of sleep.

A little preparation will be needed for this event. Friends should be notified by the teen that he will be unavailable until morning...or a number of communications may flood in with "Why aren't you answering me? Where are you?" It is recommended that both parent and teenager agree on the times. There is no doubt that a teenager who has been using their phone at night will NOT be an enthusiastically willing participant in this event. So, an attempt at proximal succession might be a better route. Try doing this for just one week. If your teen feels that he is actually getting more sleep this way, try extending it for two weeks. If another benefit can be found in realizing that the world actually keeps turning even when a text isn't immediately answered, this is improvement. If the activity can be extended beyond that time span, and the dialog with your child indicates that he is seeing benefits to this new habit, perhaps the cell phone can be left in the bedroom at night...but turned-off in the nightstand. If this can expand into a month or more, then you may have developed a very healthy habit in your teenager. And remember, the hope is that they can do the same in college and silence the communications while they are sleeping.

This not only allows for quality sleep, but time for our thoughts to catch up with our communications. I've witnessed numerous conflicts in which texts and emails were sent so quickly from one teen to another that many regretful words became part of the dialog, which may not have occurred if they had only taken some time to gain perspective and carefully chosen their content with some context. And, if a teenager is having trouble getting enough sleep or engaging in social media interactions that are emotionally distressful by using their computer in their room late at night, the same effects apply. And the off-limits times may need to include those modes of technology as well. While it is harder to sometimes remove a computer from a teenager's bedroom, the one key question that should be asked is this, "What can the teenager accomplish on the computer in their room that cannot be accomplished if the computer is down the hall in the home office, den, or study?"

Reflection on Scaffolding for Quality Sleep

Daily Time for Cell-Phone Shut-Down: _____

Daily Time for Cell-Phone Activation: _____

Ask your teenager to reflect on these questions the next day:

How many communications were actually missed through the night? _____

Did missing any of these communications negatively affect the quality of your relationships with the people who texted you? _____

Were you still able to make all of the communications you needed to the next morning? _____ **If not, what was "time sensitive" that had to be answered immediately and why?** _____

What were some of the social benefits during the activity?

_____

_____

_____

_____

After a week of adjustment without technology in the bedroom, what have you, as a parent, observed in your teen's school performance, behavior, and mood?

_____

_____

_____

_____

~ Day 30~

"RED SKY AT NIGHT"

"...Red sky at night, sailor's delight." This is a sign of smooth sailing ahead. And, while this author genuinely hopes that you encounter exactly that for the remainder of the adolescent years with your child, we all know that the reality is a series of storms on the ocean...not just one. With that in mind, it is recommended that the concepts and activities in this guide are revisited as necessary when conflict arises. Typically the place where most of us as parents fall down is in the consistency of maintaining new behaviors and keeping them in practice. This is just part of the human condition. It happens when we try to exercise, diet, quit smoking, etc. Change is difficult. And the ruts that we get into are typically created by finding a short cut to what we think is a good outcome, but isn't in the long run. So, it's only natural that it is very difficult to get out of ruts. They were developed on the principle of being quick and easy.

The goal for today is to select three to five of the past activities that you feel have the most positive effect on your relationship with your teenager and that are most likely to be of benefit in the future as well. Then, make note of the selected activities below. Set a date to consciously and physically return to those methods or behaviors and do a "self-check" at that time. This is like returning to harbor. We can replenish supplies, take refuge from the ocean, and realign our priorities. And finally, place a written memo on your calendar or in your phone schedule to provide a pleasant reminder in the midst of a very busy world. Remember? That was part of the problem identified at the beginning of the guide. The world is so complex and fast-paced today that it is easy to lose track of priorities and communication with those we love. What's to keep that from happening again? A conscious return to the practice. Hopefully with time, you may observe that the need to reference these becomes less frequent, and that the positive effects last longer in between moments.

RETURNING TO WHAT MATTERS: THE HARBOR

Activity #1 that was helpful: _____

Goal to Keep in Focus: _____

Return Date to the Harbor: _____

Activity #2 that was helpful: _____

Goal to Keep in Focus: _____

Return Date to the Harbor: _____

Activity #3 that was helpful: _____

Goal to Keep in Focus: _____

Return Date to the Harbor: _____

In Closing

It is with all the efforts put forth in creating this guidebook that the author hopes the end of this 30 day voyage has found both you and your teenager able to better weather the storms of adolescence. May calmer waters and safe harbors find you sailing with a young adult who has closer communication with his/her parents, a better understanding of self, and a firm footing on the world of adulthood.

Selected Sources and References

Baumrind, D. (1971). Current Patterns of Parental Authority. *Developmental Psychology*, 4 (1), 1-103.

Beebe, D. W. (2011). Cognitive, Behavioral, and Functional Consequences of Inadequate Sleep in Children and Adolescents. *Pediatric Clinics of North America*, 58 (3), 649-665.

Beebe, D.W., Rose, D., and Amin, R. (2010). Attention, Learning, and Arousal of Experimentally Sleep-Restricted Adolescents in a Simulated Classroom. *Journal of Adolescent Health*, 47 (5), 523-525.

Blumenfeld, W.J. and Cooper, R.M. (2010). LGBT and Allied Youth Responses to Cyberbullying: Policy Implications. *The International Journal of Critical Pedagogy,* 3 (1), 112.

Brand, S.R., Engel, S.M., Canfield, R.L., & Yehuda, R. (2006). The Effect of Maternal PTSD Following in Utero Trauma Exposure on Behavior and Temperament in the 9-Month-Old Infant. *Annals of the New York Academy of Sciences*, 1071(1), 454-458.

Bronson, P. and Merriman, A. (2009). *NurtureShock.* New York: Hatchette Book Group.

Cohen, S. (2013). The Innovation of Loneliness. *Shenkar College of Engineering and Design Project: Vimeo. http://vimeo.com/70534716.*

Connor-Smith, J.K., Compas, B.E., Wadsworth, M.E., Thomsen, A.H., and Saltzman, H. (2000). Response to Stress in Adolescence: Measurement of Coping and Involuntary Stress Responses. *Journal of Consulting and Clinical Psychology,* 28 (6), 976-992.

Currier, R. (2013). *VSAT VOICE.* June 21. *http://vsatglobalseriesblog.wordpress.com.*

DeVore, E.R., and Ginsburg, K.R., (2005). The Protective Effects of Good Parenting on Adolescents. *Current Opinion in Pediatrics,* 17 (4), 460-465.

Dewald, J. F., Meijer, A. M., Oort, F. J., Kerkhof, G. A., and Bogels, S.M. (2010). The Influence of Sleep Quality, Sleep Duration and Sleepiness on School Performance in Children and Adolescents: A Meta-Analytic Review. *Sleep Medicine Reviews*, 14, 179-189.

Di Prisco, J., and Riera, M. (2000). *Field Guide to the American Teenager.* Cambridge, MA: Perseus Books.

Dornbusch, S.M., Ritter, P.L., Leiderman, P. H., Roberts, D.F., and Fraleigh, M.J. (1987). The Relation of Parenting Style to Adolescent School Performance. *Child Development*, 58 (5), 1244-1257.

Dreikurs, R. and Soltz, V. (1990). *Children: The Challenge.* New York: Plume Group.

Erikson, E. (1968). *Identity, Youth and Crisis.* New York: Norton and Co.

Faber, A., and Mazlish, E. (2005). *How to Talk So Teens Will Listen and Listen So Teens Will Talk.* New York: Harper Collins.

Fisch, K. (2013). Did You Know 3.0. *Youtube, https://www.google.com/?gws_rd=ssl#q=karl+fisch+did+you+know+2013.*

Gallagher, R.P. (2013). National Survey of College Counseling Centers. *University of Pittsburg.*

Gardner, H. E. (2006). *Five Minds for the Future.* Boston, MA: Harvard Business School Press.

Gardner, H. E. (2006). *Frames of Mind: The Theory of Multiple Intelligence.* New York: Basic Books.

Giedd, J.N. (2012) The Digital Revolution and Adolescent Brain Evolution. *Journal of Adolescent Health,* 52 (2), 101-105.

Ginsburg, K. R. and Jablow, M. M., 2nd ed. (2011). *Building Resilience in Children and Teens: Giving Kids Roots and Wings.* Elk Grove Village, IL: American Academy of Pediatrics.

Goldstein, S., and Brooks, R.B., Eds., (2006). *Handbook of Resilience in Children.* New York: Springer-Verlag.

Goleman, D. (1995). *Emotional Intelligence: Why It Can Matter More Than IQ.* New York: Bantam Books.

Grolnick, W. S., and Ryan, R.M. (1989). Parent Styles Associated with Children's Self-Regulation and Competence in School. *Journal of Educational Psychology,* 81 (2), 143-154.

Hacker, D.J., Dunlosky, J., and Graesser, A.C. (Eds.) (1998). *Metacognition in Educational Theory and Practice.* New Jersey: Lawrence Erlbaum Associates.

Harackiewicz, J.M., Barron, Elliott, A.J., Carter, S.M., and Lehto, A.T. (1997). Predictors and Consequences of Achievement Goals in the College Classroom: Maintaining Interest and Making the Grade. *Journal of Personality and Social Psychology,* 73 (6), 1284-1295.

Harackiewicz, J.M., Barron, K.E., Tauer, J.M., and Elliott, A.J. (2002). Predicting Success in College: A Longitudinal Study of Achievement Goals and Ability Measures as Predictors of

Interest and Performance from Freshman Year through Graduation. *Journal of Educational Psychology,* 94 (3), 562-575.

Heijmans, B.T., Tobi, E.W., Stein, A.D., Putter, H., Blauw, G.J., Susser, E.S., and Lumey, L.H. (2008). Persistent epigenetic differences associated with prenatal exposure to famine in humans. *Proceedings of the National Academy of Sciences, 105*(44), 17046-17049.

Holmes, T. (1967). Holmes-Rahe Life-Stress Inventory. *Journal of Psychosomatic Research,* 11, 216.

Jantz, G.L. and McMurray, A. (2011). *The Stranger in Your House.* Colorado Springs, CO: David C. Cook Pub.

Leman, K. (2009). *The Birth Order Book, Revised and Updated.* Grand Rapids, MI: Revell.

Lewis, C.E., Siegel, J.M., Lewis, M.A. (1984). Feeling Bad: Exploring Sources of Distress Among Pre-Adolescent Children. *American Journal of Public Health,* 74 (2), 117-122.

McLeod, S. (2011). Does Hyper-Texting Lead to Stress and Depression? Or Vice Versa? *http://bigthink.com/ideas/does-hyper-texting-lead-to-stress-and-depression-or-vice-versa.*

Munsey, C. (2010): More Students-with More Serious Psychological Issues-are Showing Up at Campus Counseling Centers. *APA Monitor on Psychology,* 41 (4), 10.

McNeely, C., & Blanchard, J. (2009). *The teen years explained: A guide to healthy adolescent development.* Baltimore, MD: Center for Adolescent Health at Johns Hopkins Bloomberg School of Public Health.

Nelsen, J. (1981). *Positive Discipline.* New York: Random House.

Nelsen, J. and Lott, L. (2012). *Positive Discipline for Teenagers (Revised).* New York: Crown Publishing.

Pryor, J. H., Eagan, K., Palucki-Blake, L., Hurtado, S., Berdan, J., and Case, M.H. (2012). *The American Freshman: National Norms Fall 2012.* Los Angeles: Higher Education Research Institute, UCLA.

Punamaki,R.L., Wallenius, M., Nygard, C., Saarni, L., and Rimpela, A. (2007). Use of information and communication technology (ICT) and perceived health in adolescence: The role of sleeping habits and waking-time tiredness. *Journal of Adolescence,* 30 (4), 569-585.

Punamaki, R.L., Wallenius, M., Holtto, H., Nygard, C., and Rimpela, A. (2009). The associations between information and communication technology (ICT) and peer and parent relations in early adolescence. *International Journal of Behavioral Development,* 33 (6), 556-564.

Rideout, V., Foehr, U., and Roberts, D., (2010). Generation M: Media in the Lives of 8- to 18-Year-Olds. *The Henry J. Kaiser Family Foundation.*

Riera, M. (2003). *Staying Connected to Your Teenager.* Cambridge, MA: Perseus Publishing.

Riera, M. (2012). *Uncommon Sense for Parents with Teenagers, (3rd Ed.).* New York: Ten Speed Press.

Sapolsky, R. M. (1989). *Why Zebras Don't Get Ulcers, (3rd Ed.).* New York: Henry Holt & Co.

Schunk, D. H., and Zimmerman, B.J., (Eds.) (1994). *Self-Regulation of Learning and Performance.* New Jersey: Lawrence Erlbaum Associates.

Trice, A. (1985). An Academic Locus of Control Scale for college students. *Perceptual and Motor Skills*, 61, 1043-1046.

Trice, A. et al. (1987). Concurrent Validity of the Academic Locus of Control Scale. *Educational and Psychological Measurement, 47,* 483-486.

Walker, J. (2005). Adolescent Stress and Depression. *Extension Center for Youth Development,* University of Minnesota Online Extension.

Walsh, D. (2004). *Why Do They Act That Way? A Survival Guide to the Adolescent Brain for You and Your Teen.* New York: Free Press.

Wolfson, A. R., and Carskadon, M. A. (1998). Sleep Schedules and Daytime Functioning in Adolescents. *Child Development*, 69 (4), 875-887.

Wong, M. M. (2008). Perceptions of Parental Involvement and Autonomy Support: Their Relations with Self-Regulation, Academic Performance, Substance Use and Resilience among Adolescents. *North American Journal of Psychology,* 10 (3), 497-518.

Yehuda, R., Engel, S.M., Brand, S.R., Seckl, J., Marcus, S.M., & Berkowitz, G.S. (2005). Transgenerational effects of posttraumatic stress disorder in babies of mothers exposed to the World Trade Center attacks during pregnancy. *The Journal of Clinical Endocrinology & Metabolism*, *90*(7), 4115-4118.

Zimmerman, B.J., and Schunk, D.H. (Eds.), (2001). *Self-Regulated Learning and Academic Achievement, (2nd Ed.).* New Jersey: Lawrence Erlbaum Associates.

www.ingramcontent.com/pod-product-compliance
Lightning Source LLC
Chambersburg PA
CBHW070144290526
45789CB00002B/616